A Jungian Understanding of Symbolic Function and Forms

I0095091

The purpose of this book is to clarify the function of the symbol and its place at the juncture of psychoanalysis and other social sciences, where the singular and the collective intersect and whose laws are identical.

The debate between Freud and Jung about the symbol is well known; by examining the points of contradiction between their respective approaches, this book seeks to place them in fruitful tension, rather than categorical opposition and explore their similarities and differences. In later chapters, the author further analyses the function of the symbol in relation to the topics of myth, anthropology and dreams.

This thoughtful book will appeal to those interested and involved in analytical psychology and psychoanalysis, as well as psychiatrists and psychologists.

Dominique Boukhabza is a psychiatrist and psychoanalyst. She has published: *La lettre du rêve, un lecteur pour la psychose,* erès/Arcanes, 2012, *Le cas Jung, Aperçu sur la face psychotique du transfert,* Anthropos Economica, 2017, and many articles. She is the president of the association *Lien de la lettre.*

A Jungian Understanding of Symbolic Function and Forms

The Dream Series

Dominique Boukhabza

Routledge
Taylor & Francis Group

LONDON AND NEW YORK

First published 2023
by Routledge
4 Park Square, Milton Park, Abingdon, Oxon OX14 4RN

and by Routledge
605 Third Avenue, New York, NY 10158

Routledge is an imprint of the Taylor & Francis Group, an informa business

British Library Cataloguing-in-Publication Data
A catalogue record for this book is available from the British Library

Library of Congress Cataloguing-in-Publication Data
Names: Boukhabza, Dominique, author.
Title: A Jungian understanding of symbolic function and forms : in search of symbols / Dominique Boukhabza.
Description: Abingdon, Oxon ; New York, NY : Routledge, 2024. | Includes bibliographical references and index. |
Summary: "The purpose of this book is to clarify the function of the symbol and its place at the juncture of psychoanalysis and other social sciences, where the singular and the collective intersect and whose laws are identical. The debate between Freud and Jung about the symbol is well known; by examining the points of contradiction between their respective approaches, this book seeks to place them in fruitful tension, rather than categorical opposition and explore their similarities and differences. In later chapters, the author further analyses the function of the symbol in relation to the topics of myth, anthropology, and dreams. This thoughtful book will appeal to those interested and involved in analytical psychology and psychoanalysis, as well as psychiatrists and psychologists"-- Provided by publisher.
Identifiers: LCCN 2023009425 (print) | LCCN 2023009426 (ebook) |
ISBN 9781032448022 (hardback) | ISBN 9781032448015 (paperback) |
ISBN 9781003373988 (ebook)
Subjects: LCSH: Symbolism (Psychology) | Jungian psychology.
Classification: LCC BF175.5.S95 B68 2024 (print) | LCC BF175.5.S95 (ebook) |
DDC 150.19/54--dc23/eng/20230515
LC record available at https://lccn.loc.gov/2023009425
LC ebook record available at https://lccn.loc.gov/2023009426

ISBN: 978-1-032-44802-2 (hbk)
ISBN: 978-1-032-44801-5 (pbk)
ISBN: 978-1-003-37398-8 (ebk)

DOI: 10.4324/b23380

Typeset in Times New Roman
by MPS Limited, Dehradun

Contents

Introduction

The meaning of the term "symbol", its nature as well as its function, needs to be clarified in the field of psychoanalysis and in relation to the other social sciences: semiotics and linguistics, anthropology and philosophy, with which psychoanalysis maintains essential ties. Symbols are at the very heart of these ties. The laws that govern the formation of symbols in the social group must be recognised as identical to those that guide the subject's own path. Therefore, our work will focus on symbols as they appear in the field of analysis in dreams, myths, symptoms and delusions but also on symbols as the intersection between the individual and the social group. Symbols belong to both the individual and the group and are what draw the intersection between psychoanalysis and the related sciences.

The path of dreams, as explored in our clinical practice, has led us to an understanding that includes, yet also extends, the Freudian conception. Dreams, activated by transference, are connected as series. Each dream represents a link belonging to one or more sequences that generate a network. This network develops through the work of the dream and its task of symbolisation. This work is required precisely from the points where, for the subject, the symbol is lacking. This latter aspect orientates our interest in Jung's personal trajectory and his works, often side-lined too quickly by Freudian psychoanalysts after his split with Freud. Jung's contribution to dreams, symbols and what he calls the individuation process, demonstrated by the chains of dreams, sheds light on the processes of symbolisation. In our approach to the Freud–Jung debate, we prefer to choose tension rather than opposition. Too many controversies, often irrelevant, clutter the field of psychoanalysis due to insufficient development of contradictory points. We will, therefore, try to show, first of all, how the Freudian and Jungian concepts each refer to exact, yet partial, approaches to symbols and their formation, due to their different starting points. Jung's thinking is based on, and remains close to, the issue of psychosis. Jung, as Bleuler's assistant, participated in the work on dementia praecox and its characteristic dissociation. Schizophrenia, this new name coined by Bleuler, became a major concept in psychiatric nosography. This starting point made the symbol, this critical

DOI: 10.4324/b23380-1

associative element, one of Jung's privileged topics. His approach to symbols is fundamentally collective. The theory of archetypes is to be understood, as we shall see as "collective" traces of the symbolic function, and as the particular place held by the notion of God. However, the work of Bleuler and his team also owes much to Freudian thinking on repression and the associative technique, exported and re-elaborated in the concept of schizophrenia. Freudian thinking, for its part, is anchored around the question of the "father" from primary identification to the formation of the Ego-ideal, which is also the matrix of repression and symptom; Freud's symbol, that of the dream as well as that of the symptom, privileges the link to repression. Freud's thinking starts from the individual and neurosis. The collective symbolism of dreams, nevertheless, has a place, yet this place is more one of accessory. The Ego-ideal, above all, receives a collective interpretation; its function as a pivot of the organisation in crowds is masterfully demonstrated without the analytical institutions themselves, unfortunately managed to detach from such an organisation.

Moreover, psychoanalysis could not avoid referring to the social sciences as it developed. Freud and Jung relied on the anthropology of their time: Freud with *Totem and Taboo* and its subsequent re-elaborations—*Collective Psychology and Analysis of the Ego* and *The Ego and the Id*—and Jung with the subject/object lack of differentiation and the mystical participation of Lévy-Bruhl. Each of them gave their version of how to escape narcissism, based on myths and symbols. Lacan himself referred to the work of Lévi-Strauss to support the primacy of the symbolic function for the individual as well as for the social group. The individual and the group are governed by the same principles; myths and dreams equally proceed from the human drive. The work of Ernst Cassirer, less known than that of Lévi-Strauss, further clarifies the characteristics of mythical thought and notes its persistence despite the development of culture. His *Philosophy of Symbolic Forms* develops the links between myth, language and knowledge as distinct symbolic forms that evolve together. Cassirer does not refer to psychoanalysis, which was contemporaneous with his work, but his thought seems very close to psychoanalysis in that it is interested in symbolic "forms" and in the interrelationships between these forms and, even though this word is not used much by him, he is interested in symbolisation as a process. We will focus on this process of symbolisation because it is at the same time a process of subjectivisation.

Chapter 1

The Freud–Jung debate on symbols

Freud's *Interpretation of Dreams* was published in 1899. In the preface to the second edition, in 1908, Freud explicitly presented the work as a piece of his self-analysis and his reaction to the death of his father. The distortion of dreams, according to Freud, resulted from the action of censorship but also from a second factor: the symbolism of dreams. In the preface to the third edition, published in 1911, he emphasised the importance of the symbolism of dreams and considered, in later editions, a more thorough study of the links between dreams and mental illnesses, with this latter point remaining unresolved. However, alongside the symbolism of dreams, Freud used the term "symbolic" in another way. The term "symbolic" referred, in a general way, to the relationship between the manifest content of a behaviour, a thought or a word and its latent meaning. Following Freud, several authors (Rank, Sachs, Ferenczi and Jones) affirmed that in psychoanalysis one can only speak of symbolism when the symbolised element is unconscious. The other meaning of symbolism in Freud's works was connected to the question of the symptom.

As early as 1900, Jung had read *the Interpretation of Dreams,* but it was not until 1903, during his work with word associations that he fully understood it. It then appeared to him that the absence of associative response or its late appearance could be connected to the repression mechanism introduced by Freud.[1] From the outset, the place of sexuality in the constitution of neuroses seemed to him to be exaggerated, all the more so because, as we shall see, the term sexuality did not have for him the same meaning it had for Freud, notably in its relationship to infantile sexuality. Nevertheless, at a time when Freudian works were still controversial, Jung supported him in his own work.[2]

Jung and schizophrenia

Schizophrenia is at the root of Jungian thought on symbols. The associative disorders of schizophrenia and its characteristic hyper-symbolism were to pave the way for the study of symbols.

DOI: 10.4324/b23380-2

Jung took his first steps in psychiatry under the direction of Bleuler at the Burghölzli Clinic. Bleuler enjoyed great fame at the time because of his work on psychosis. He introduced the term "schizophrenia" which replaced Kraepelin's term "dementia praecox". This latter term designated a mental illness characterised by a progressive evolution towards a state of psychic weakening accompanied by profound affective disorders. Within this term, Kraepelin distinguished three clinical forms: hebephrenia, catatonia and a paranoid form characterised by the importance of delusions. But, according to him, it was not so much a dementia in the sense of a mental weakening, more a *dissociation* of the psychic life which lost its coherence, or a sort of disintegration of the personality. Furthermore, it is precisely the notion of dissociation which was implied in the very concept of "schizophrenia", the term by which Bleuler proposed to designate the group Kraepelin had originally termed "dementia praecox". For Bleuler, the patients were not demented but suffered from a process of dislocation that disintegrated their *associative capacity,* plunging them into an "autistic" life where ideas and feelings were the symbolic expression of unconscious complexes.

Association tests

Bleuler therefore introduced the test of verbal associations at the Burghölzli because, for him, the fundamental symptom of schizophrenia was *the loosening of associations.* He entrusted this work to Jung who worked with Frank Riklin using the word association experiment of Wilhelm Wundt, the founder of experimental psychology. Wundt himself had taken up the test from Francis Galton in order to establish experimentally the laws of associations of ideas.[3] In addition, Kraepelin was able to distinguish between various associative modalities, notably those based on sense and those based on sound and began to apply the association test to the main mental diseases. The test consisted of pronouncing a series of carefully chosen words and addressed to the patient who had to respond each time with the first word that came into his mind. The reaction time, which was noted, was shown to be prolonged in the presence of a "complex". The term "complex", introduced by Ziehen, was taken up by Jung to designate a psychic fragment with a strong emotional charge, originating in the unconscious and consisting of a central element and a large number of secondary associations. It was this emotional charge that slowed down the associative reaction, or even made it impossible in some cases, notably in dementia praecox. Consciousness is considered to have a *natural* tendency to dissociate. This dissociability is reinforced by the effect of psychic contents which, following traumatic events, have been rejected into the unconscious where they lead an autonomous existence. Jung called these contents "affective complexes". Therefore, Jung applied the association test method to his work on dementia praecox.

While he was, at the same time, greatly influenced by Freud's work on free association, in his introduction to the *Psychology of Dementia Praecox,*[4] affirming the essential role of clinical experience, Jung was already eager to show his independence and to make a distinction between what he received from Freud's works, especially the mechanisms of dreams and hysteria, and what differentiated him from them, essentially the role of infantile sexual trauma.

Dementia praecox: a dissociation

In the first part of his work, Jung connected the development of associations in dementia praecox, particularly those based on assonance, to that of dreams. Other similarities were the predominance of symbols and the production of neologisms. The latters, like linguistic roots, are neither verbs nor nouns but serve to condensate a whole thought process. The concept of condensation is one of the mechanisms of dream work isolated by Freud, but in the case of dementia praecox, the condensation of neologisms shows the interruption of the process of symbolisation that, on the contrary, dreams would be able to start up again.

Jung also analysed Otto Gross' understanding of the psychology of dementia praecox. Gross proposed to call it *dementia sejunctiva* because of the *sejunctio*, meaning the disjunction of consciousness. The term *sejunctio,* borrowed from Wernicke, was, according to Jung, synonymous with that of dissociation used by the French school (Binet, Janet). However, this term more clearly evoked the cut that took place. Dissociation implied that one or more series of representations split and free themselves from the hierarchy of the consciousness. This was what Freud and Breuer demonstrated with hysteria, but Gross also applied it to dementia praecox since, for him, the disintegration of consciousness consisted of simultaneous but separate series of associations. When the connections between these series are broken, the disintegration of consciousness appears, with its automatic manifestations, hallucinations, impulses and blockades, enabling several series of associations to take place in consciousness simultaneously. Among these series, there is normally one which has to become the carrier of the continuity of consciousness while the other series remain unconscious. If an element from an unconscious series of associations is suddenly inserted into the continuity of the dominant series, it is perceived as having been projected from outside to inside consciousness, this being the case with hallucinations, such as hearing "voices". Thus the roots of all automatic phenomena would be found in the unconscious groupings of associations.

For Jung, the dissociation of consciousness is the result of an absence of connections between the different complexes of representations whose cement is in fact constituted by a determined *affect.* What puzzles him is the idea of a series of synchronous but independent associations. In hysteria, he says, it is the opposite, even if the series seems to be completely separate, we always find, in a hidden place, a bridge that goes from one series to the other. But isn't it this untraceable bridge that makes psychosis specific? Actually, Jung says, as early as 1893, Freud showed how an unbearable effect can trigger a hallucinatory delusion representing a kind of compensation for unsatisfied desires.[5] With regard to a paranoid delusion that could be classified in the group of dementia praecox,[6] Freud was able to establish a parallel between the mechanisms of the delusion and those at the roots of conversion hysteria. For Freud, this paranoid delusion is to be included in the group known as *defence psychoneuroses*, under the heading of repression, with the content of the repression giving the symptoms their form. The ideas that are incompatible with consciousness, because of the displeasure they arouse, have been repressed and then manifest themselves. These repressed elements therefore determine the content of the delusions or hallucinations. However, Jung insists, we do not see why, in this case, dementia praecox appears rather than hysteria. Moreover, hysteria is characterised by an extreme lability of symptoms, whereas paranoid delusions are very stable and resistant. The affective accentuation of the delusions leads to their systematic reproduction, hence the isolation of the patients due to their inability to share their emotions.

Here we can see the problem of libido and narcissism that will later be one of the elements of Jung's theoretical conflict with Freud. For Freud, the distinction between transference psychoneuroses and narcissistic psychoneuroses is established according to the criterion of the accessibility or not to transference. The starting point is the psychic conflict. Depending on the outcome of this conflict, displacement or metaphorization, i.e. obsessional representations or hysterical conversion will occur. But, in the case of psychosis, everything happens as if the representation had never reached the ego. There is a cut: a *"sejunctio"*. Symbolism thus appears to us as an attempt at *"rejunctio"*. For us, that also means that rather than a representation, a trace has remained.

The thought connected to the repressed complex, Jung continues, can be disguised in similar forms, either by assonance or by resemblance *via* the visual image as in dreams, as Freud indicates in the *Interpretation of Dreams*. In some cases, it can manifest itself symbolically, as in the example cited by Freud in *Psychopathology of Everyday Life*: *a-liquis*.[7] But of course, it is the construction of the dream that provides the most striking examples of symbolic expression of the repressed complex. Analogical image expression as manifested in the dream (and Jung again quotes *The Interpretation of Dreams*) is also very important for the psychology of dementia praecox, given the prevalence of this symbolic expression in its delusional manifestations.

At this point in his writings, Jung inserts the account of a dream that is attributed to a friend but which we later learn is his own[8]:

In the dream, he sees horses being hoisted to an indeterminate height. One of them, a sturdy bay horse, harnessed with straps, is being lifted like a pack when one of the ropes breaks, causing the horse to fall back in the street; he thinks it is dead but the horse gets up and gallops away. It is dragging a heavy tree *trunk* behind him; but despite this, he is moving very fast and risks causing an accident. Then a rider on a small horse comes along and gets in front of the horse to slow him down. Then a carriage comes along, moving at walking pace in front of him and slowing down the horse even more. Jung says to himself: "It's all right now, the danger is over".

Jung's associations: horses work in the mines (*Berg-Werke*). *Berg* (mountain) and *Werke* (work) are the starting point for the associations. *Berg* talks about his desire to go to the mountains and to travel, but his wife is pregnant so they cannot travel. They had to give up a trip to America and he thinks of skyscrapers and their height. *Berg-Werke* could therefore be understood as elevating oneself through work, with the word used as a symbol of this idea. The rope that breaks, letting the horse fall, probably expresses a disappointment but we don't know exactly what it is. The horse galloping off again indicates that it has not let itself be knocked down. He now remembers that a second horse helped the first to pull the tree trunk. This second horse could be his wife. The bay horse is galloping, reminiscent of a painting by Welti in which horses are galloping on a ledge where among them is a horse in rut. The painting also shows a couple in bed. The symbol of the horse thus takes on a sexual meaning. Jung fears that his fiery temperament will drive him too fast. Indeed, the rider on the small horse comes alongside and moderates his pace. The little horse looks like a child's horse. It also reminds him of a pregnant woman he had seen as a child, whose prominent belly had made him wonder whether she was wearing a small horse under her clothes. On the other hand, pregnancy imposes restraint on the man, as is also indicated by the occurrence of the carriage, which he remembers as being full of children. We are thus in the presence, Jung tells us, of two complexes, one relating to professional ambition, the other to more personal matters of a sexual nature; but because of *the lack of sensitivity to differences*[9] which reigns in dreams, the contents of the two complexes merge into a form which then becomes a symbolic form. When one complex is excited, the conscious association is disturbed and becomes superficial by flight or inhibition of attention to the autonomous complex. The autonomous complex can only signal its existence through blurred symptomatic associations which then have a symbolic character; they lack the full investment of attention required by the ego complex. Symbols are only secondary associations to an idea, which cloud that idea rather than illuminate it.

Jung used the association test to show the impact of a complex on the different associative chains in dementia praecox. Inductive words were chosen in particular among the neologisms. He produced a case study of a 60-year-old patient, a former seamstress, who had spent 20 years in the clinic. In this patient, as is usually seen in dementia praecox, Jung noted a significant prevalence of unconscious complexes, infiltrating the bulk of her associations. Jung also noted, without, unfortunately, elaborating on the subject, that most of her delusions were drawn from dreams. He deduced three major complexes in the patient through a focus on the associations. There were a complex of personal greatness, a complex of prejudice, and an erotic complex, which took a back seat to the other two.

The patient's discourse is peppered with numerous neologisms that she herself describes as "words of power" (*Machtwörter*). The intelligibility of the delusion is demonstrated by the associations produced by the patient from the elements of the delusion, as well as the neologisms that were used as inductive words:

For example, the patient said: "I am Socrates". Using Socrates as an inducing word, came in association:

> Pupil—books—wisdom—modesty—no words to express this wisdom—is the highest ground-pedestal—his teachings-had to die because of wicked men—falsely accused—sublimest sublimity—self-satisfied-that is all Socrates—the fine learned world—never cut a thread—I was the best dressmaker, never left a bit of cloth on the floor—fine world of art—fine professorship—is doubloon—25 francs—that is the highest-prison—slandered by wicked men—unreason—cruelty depravity—brutality.[10]

Jung analysed the patient's associations as follows:

> The explanation of her stereotypy "I am Socrates" or "I am Socratic" is that she is the "best dressmaker" who "never cut a thread" and "never left a bit of cloth on the floor." She is an "artist," a "professor" in her line. She is martyred, she is not recognized as the owner of the world, she is considered ill, which is a "slander." She is "wise" and "modest," she has achieved "the highest." All these things are analogies of the life and death of Socrates. She therefore wishes to say: "I am like Socrates, and I suffer like him." With a certain poetic licence, such as appears also in moments of strong affect, she says outright: "I am Socrates." The really pathological element is that she is so identified with Socrates that she can no longer get away from him; she takes the identification at its face value and regards the metonymy as so real that she expects everybody to understand it.[11]

Jung thus points out the identification with Socrates but refers to it as an insufficiency of the capacity to distinguish between two representations, an indication of the work of the unconscious with its capacity to operate condensations, thanks to the vagueness of the representations which occurs particularly in dreams. For Jung, the necessary condition for this condensation is therefore what he calls the blurring of representations already mentioned above, allowing the formation of the symbol and the lack of sensitivity to difference to be the principle of symbolic associations. The complex works according to the law of analogy; it is completely freed from the authority of the ego complex. In the case of this patient, the analysis, Jung tells us, was conducted exactly like the analysis of a dream. The associations obtained in this case, using this method, are grouped by him around three main themes, which manifest, in all cases the satisfaction of desires, in the form of a grandeur complex, a prejudice complex and a sexual complex. Alongside these three complexes, a critical instance persists which occasionally brings the patient back to reason, sometimes manifesting itself ironically.

This "insufficiency of the ability to distinguish between two representations" is, for us, *the impossibility of perceiving an identifying trait.* The patient identifies herself with Socrates on the basis of at least two traits:

First trait: she is the best seamstress, an artist, a sage or a teacher in her field.
Second trait: she was, like Socrates, slandered and imprisoned.

Except that instead of seeing common features between Socrates and her own life, she *is* Socrates. The trait on which the identification is based is elided. Identification as identification with a trait cannot be perceived as such. The identification with Socrates is realised in much the same way as a dream would realise it, condensing the dreamer and Socrates by making Socrates the main character of the dream. The discovery of this identification could be expected from the analysis of a dream, which is however excluded in the case of delusion. One could say that Socrates is there as a symbol of both wisdom and prejudice. This point is important because it is precisely what will serve as the basis for the Jungian interpretation of dreams, that is, the identification with great symbols conveyed by civilisations rather than on the identification of a trait transmitted in a filiation for example.

In a later work on psychosis, Jung was interested in the symbolism of schizophrenia and its connection with mythology. In schizophrenia, indeed, one finds a number of typical creations with obvious analogies to mythological productions. The question is whether the materials compared are similar or not. Schizophrenia, above all, presents a large number of collective symbols, because, as Jung tells us, it dislocates the foundations of the psyche, which explains the overflow of collective symbols that form the basic structure of the personality.[12] The schizophrenic mental state, in which this archaic material predominates, has all the characteristics of what Jung calls a "great dream", i.e. it has the same properties that were attributed, in primitive civilisations, to a magical ritual. In another work,[13] Jung used these manifestations of the collective symbolism of schizophrenia to develop the notion of archetype. It is the material present in schizophrenia that first gave him the idea of a deeper stratum of the unconscious. This material appears in myths, tales, fantasies and dreams as well as in the visions and the delusional productions of psychosis.

To summarise, schizophrenia deals with the same symbolic material as that of mythology, which is also present in dreams. This collective symbolism forms the basic structure of the personality, the deepest stratum of the unconscious. In schizophrenia, this material overflows due to the dislocation of the foundations of the psyche. But what does this dislocation consist of? Is it equivalent to dissociation, a *sejunctio*? Is the hyper-symbolism of schizophrenia then an attempt at *rejunctio* in which the subject is eliminated? The seamstress is not "like Socrates", an unjustly maligned sage, she *is* Socrates. The symbolic material does not serve to represent the subject, it is the subject. Of this relationship between the subject, elided and the symbol, Jung's book *Metamorphoses of the Libido and its Symbols*[14] is the next milestone.

The Metamorphoses of the Libido and its Symbols

The *Metamorphoses* were built on the presentation of a case, that of Miss Miller, published by the Geneva psychiatrist Flournoy. Using extremely detailed clinical material, it was an opportunity for Jung to develop a very dense analysis of myths taken from very diverse cultural spheres, such as Greco-Roman and Egyptian antiquity, Christianity, the cult of Mithras, the Indian Upanishads, etc., which he related to these clinical elements. The aim was to demonstrate the convergence of these myths as tools for symbolising the essential features of human problems. Jung multiplies the examples and manages, from this narrow starting point, to produce (at least for the last edition which includes the additions of the successive editions and an equally abundant iconography) a work of more than 700 pages. Myth also attracted the attention of Freud, Abraham, Rank and other analysts of the time. Nevertheless, Jung, beyond the light that the knowledge of myths can shed on the human being, extracted, from the study of myths, a method and the analysis of the case of Miss Miller, produced of course from a writing, that of Flournoy, constituted its outline.

For Jung, therefore, the study of the unconscious sheds light on historical and symbolic issues, with the reverse also being true. There is an analogy between the mythological thought of antiquity and infantile or primitive thought or dream thought. This leads him to consider a correspondence between the ontogenetic development of the individual and the psychological phylogenesis of the human race, which, as Jung points out, coincided with Freud's thinking. It is not the stories of any event that are transmitted through myths, but only those that translate a general, specific idea of the human condition, those that allow man to reflect on his own condition. For the psychology of groups, typical myths are a way of elaborating complexes. This is the case with the myth of Oedipus for the Greeks, but also with that of Faust for the Germans. *Directed thought, from which scientific thought is derived, and primitive, associative thought, are opposed to each other.* Directed thought is the prerogative of the conscious part of the psyche. It is through imaginative thought that the connection between directed, conscious thought and its most primitive layers is established. Man's fantasies reflect individual conflict as much as collective, archaic themes.

Jung, therefore, took over the study of the case brought by Flournoy, that of Miss Miller, a young American travelling through Europe. He focuses in particular on the study of two dream poems produced by the young girl as well as on some of her visions. The first dream poem is *The Hymn to Creation*. This poem arose in Miss Miller's dream during a night on a boat, as if in response to a voice that seemed to be her mother's, saying: "When the morning stars sang in chorus". This poem had the aspect of a religious hymn, a hymn to divine creation, born unconsciously, which reminded her of various passages in the *Book of Job*,[15] showing a God who was both creator and destroyer. Let us quote the first stanza:

When the Eternal first made Sound
A myriad ears sprang out to hear,
And throughout all the Universe
There rolled an echo deep and clear:
"All glory to the God of Sound!"

For Jung, the *poem is a substitute for an erotic problem.* In this case, it would be a love attraction for a naval officer who she had briefly seen the day before, singing on the deck of the boat. The nocturnal singer, meeting the paternal imago, Jung continues, had become a creator; he had become a god of sound, light and love[16]: "Obviously, it is a question of the displacement of the libido onto a symbolic object that has become a sort of substitute". It is *in this sense that we must understand the term metamorphosis of the libido.* God thus comes here as a substitute for an erotic problem in the background of the father complex, a theory Freud would easily have agreed with. Between the normal psychic metamorphosis that culturally transposes natural instinctive forces (for example in art) and this one, a difference emerges, marked by the seal of repression, in the intentional (unconscious) omission of the triggering event (the singer). The repression, assimilated here into an illegitimate conflict, provokes by regression the reanimation of the paternal imago and its divine projection. God is a complex of an archetypal nature representing a certain amount of energy (the libido) appearing in the form of a projection, that is, according to Jung's later denomination, a collective archetype and therefore an unconscious psychic formation. It is a psychic being, that is, to be differentiated from the concept of a metaphysical God.[17] It is connected to the paternal imago but also, in the oldest religions, to *the maternal imago,* in the form of theriomorphic representations which are very frequent. In contrast, there are few theriomorphic elements in Christianity, with the exception of a few remains such as the dove and the fish.

Later on, Miss Miller, continuing her journey, is later on a night train to Paris. She sees a moth flying towards the light in the compartment. Immediately, as she tries to go back to sleep, in conditions similar to the occurrence of *The Hymn to Creation*, in a hypnagogic state, a new poem comes to her, entitled *The Moth's Song*. It is about a moth that, like its fellow moths, longs for the sun and approaches the light until it perishes. Jung, leaning on Miss Miller's associations compares the moth's longing for the sun to that of man's longing for God. He considers that, as in *The Hymn of Creation*, this poem translates the transformation of her desire for man into a desire for God, represented here by the sun star and renews the symbolic equation also illustrated by President Schreber: Father = God = Sun.

Moreover, the *Metamorphoses* discusses the case of the Solar Phallus Man, the Schwyzer case, on which Jung worked with Honneger[18] in 1909:

> I once came across the following hallucination in a schizophrenic patient: he told me he could see an erect phallus on the sun. When he moved his head from side to side, he said, the sun's phallus moved with it, and that was where the wind came from. This bizarre notion remained unintelligible to me for a long time, until I got to know the visions in the Mithraic liturgy.[19]

Jung doesn't see, in this analogy, the fact of inherited representations but that of a *functional disposition to reproduce similar representations*. It is important to emphasise this point. It is this "disposition", which touches on the human ability to produce symbols from what constitutes the universe, that Jung will later name archetype. This disposition is accompanied by a force or an energy:

> The well-known fact that in worshipping the sun's strength we pay homage to the great generative force of Nature is the plainest possible evidence—if evidence were still needed—that in God we honour the energy of the archetype.[20]

This energy of the archetype is the libido. The symbolisation of the libido takes place through three different forms of comparison:

The *analogical comparison*, e.g. "like the sun".

The *causative comparison*. This is comparison by ways of the object where the libido is designated by its object, e.g. the beneficial sun, or it is comparison by ways of the subject where the libido is designated by its instrument or analogon, e.g. the phallus or the snake.

Finally, there is the *comparison of activity* where the *tertium comparationis* is activity. For example, the libido is dangerous like the lion or lustful like the donkey, etc.

The vector of symbolisation is thus a comparison; it is the support of total or partial identification with a trait from the drive life, either directly or displaced. The symbol is a way of speaking about it *that bypasses the vagaries of singularity*. This is important because it shows how the symbol is connected

by Jung to the drive life without this drive life having to be sheltered by the
body of any individual.

> Symbols are not signs, nor allegories replacing something known, they seek
> to announce a little known or even unknown state of affairs. The *tertium
> comparationis* of all these symbols is the libido.[21]

Symbols are neither allegory nor *semeion* (sign). They are the image of a
content that largely transcends consciousness; they are an indeterminate, even
equivocal, expression indicating something not yet elucidated. Symbols represent a psychological truth and they do not come from outside. Among the
most common symbols are the theriomorphic representations which represent
animal instinctivity in a state of repression. They frequently appear in
dreams. Among the anthropomorphic representations, the hero has a special
place for Jung. The myth of the hero will later be given a leading role in
Jungian works, embodying the struggle for independence and emancipation
from the mother. The theme of the hero appears in Miss Miller's work in the
form of a hypnagogic reverie, after an evening of anguish followed by visions:
first a sphinx, then a person, an Aztec, similar to the sculptures in Mexican
monuments. Miss Miller mentioned, in fact, a childhood interest in Aztec
fragments and Inca history.

As a result of this vision, a name is formed "piece by piece". This name is
Chi-wan-to-pel. This character is considered by Jung as the primitive aspect
of the father, a virile ideal and an analogon of the naval officer of the hymn
to creation, i.e. a hero. The name Chiwantopetl evokes for Miss Miller that
of Popocatepetl, the volcano of the Andes, which Jung links to the English
word "to pop" which can mean, especially for children, the act of defeca-
tion. Thus the appearance of the character of Chiwantopel is similar to an
anal birth. This appearance is followed by a swarm of characters: horses
appear and a battle is fought. Then appears "a city of dreams", a maternal
symbol for Jung, who once again draws on abundant sources from the Old
Testament and Egyptian antiquity. The connection to the mother is manifested here.

Jung took this opportunity to develop his concept for the prohibition of
incest. For him, the incestuous desire is above all that of becoming again a
child and of returning to the mother in order to be born by her again. This
is undoubtedly one of the ways for incest to manifest itself. The prohibition
of incest thus intervenes here as an obstacle to this return *in utero,* and it is
indeed the *raison d'être* for the rebirth myths to allow *the libido to flow into
new forms* and to block the way to true incest. This clarifies the role of
symbols for Jung, as the role of derivation of the libido and of channelling.
Symbols and symbolisation are civilising through their action of channelling the libido. The libido *channelled in symbols* is what blocks the way to
incest.

The symbols act as transformers, their function being to convert libido from a "lower" into a "higher" form. This function is so important that feeling accords it the highest values. The symbol works by suggestion; that is to say, it carries conviction and at the same time expresses the content of that conviction. It is able to do this because of the numen, the specific energy stored up in the archetype. Experience of the archetype is not only impressive, it seizes and possesses the whole personality, and is naturally productive of faith. "Legitimate" faith must always rest on experience.[22]

The energy of the archetype constitutes its convincing force, the one that seizes by impressing its force of truth, the truth of the experience of the unconscious.

Let us now return to Miss Miller. In her next vision, the forest is the scene where the dramatic representation of Chiwantopel's end takes place. Chiwantopel appears on horseback, the horse is also a symbol of the mother and the hero-horse combination represents the idea of man and the instinctual sphere he is subjected to. An Indian approaches the hero and is ready to shoot an arrow at him. But Chiwantopel gestures that he will uncover his chest, as if to incite his attacker to shoot, in a posture of pride. The hero, the ideal image of the dreamer, shows that he is willing to die. He does not fear death.

But for Jung, however, the arrow does not come from outside forces. It is Chiwantopel himself who is chasing and martyring himself; he is his own executioner. The wound indicates the entry into a state of introversion, as is the case whenever a new orientation or adaptation becomes necessary. This movement is that of *regression* which mobilises the archetypal constellations corresponding to the situation encountered. But in Miss Miller's vision, the character of Chiwantopel is not hit by the arrow. The sacrifice, which will become a major Jungian concept, does not take place. The abandonment of the attachment to the mother cannot be carried out. The abandonment of the maternal bond is what is at stake. Indeed, the appearance of visions and dreams coincides for Miss Miller with a great journey, the trip to Europe which, for this young American, takes her out of her childhood environment. For Jung, it is this struggle for independence, initiated by the journey, that should be placed on the fantasy of the shooting arrow. But in Miss Miller's case, this very thought of the struggle for independence is not realised. Chiwantopel, who plays her part, is neither wounded nor killed. He realises what Miss Miller is avoiding but does not go through with it: he offers himself to the deadly arrow but his assailant then disappears. Next, Chiwantopel begins a monologue, recalling his long journeys in search of someone to love and the conquests he made along the way, none of which have satisfied him. It is to a mother's love that he remains attached and this is the reason for his failure. Miss Miller, through her imaginary identification with Chiwantopel, achieves in fantasy a scenario that concerns her.

For Jung, as we have said, regression is indispensable as a "structural" moment because it is regression that allows the mobilisation of archetypal material, which produces an obstacle to incest in itself. But, on the other hand, the father himself is an obstacle to regression and this is the meaning of the fight against him.[23] The symbols have the effect of preventing the regressing libido from placing itself on the mother's body. It is therefore from both parents that the threatening danger comes: firstly from the father because he makes regression impossible and secondly from the mother because she absorbs into herself and holds back the libido. For Miss Miller, according to Jung, the choice of a male hero condenses the figuration of a masculine ideal and what Jung will designate as the manifestation of the animus, the masculine part of the woman and the residue of an identification with the father, and, therefore, both an ideal object and an identification with this object. Its convocation by the unconscious signals the fact that the conflict has not reached consciousness. The integration of the unconscious has not been achieved and manifests itself even more violently because it has been ignored. This is a major thesis of Jungian thought and has a particular relevance for us in the field of the psychoses.

As Chiwantopel's monologue continues with the evocation of an impossible beloved, a viper appears and puts an end to the drama with its deadly sting, striking first his horse and then the hero himself. The latter dies, calling out to the one who would understand him *(analogon* of the mother) for whom he has kept his body inviolate. Jung emphasises the feminine character of this last word. The snake personifies the threatening aspect of the conflict and the hero's death, maintained in this phantasmatic context and signals Miss Miller's inability to elaborate, let alone act on, the problem of sacrifice suggested by Chiwantopel's fantasy. Sacrifice, when it is agreed upon and chosen, is no longer destruction but metamorphosis. The sacrifice of the horse symbolises the abandonment of instinctual tendencies, whereas that of the hero is one of a higher ethical value and implies the renunciation of being simply a self, in order to reach the Jungian Self, the world of the unconscious. In this sense, the hero appears as "more" than human, divine in the Jungian sense. The hero is the actor of the metamorphosis of God in man.

Miss Miller is unable to analyse the conflict that runs through her and which is expressed and symbolised in the terms of her fantasy. One might indeed ask why this symbolisation does not produce the expected effects. It seems that it is the absence of elaboration from the symbols that is the cause. It is this absence of elaboration and consequently the absence of *connection* with the world of instincts that exposes her, according to Jung, to the risk of alienation by splitting, in other words to schizophrenia. At that time, Jung considered that the presence of mythological inner images was a sign of a loosening of the phylogenetic layers of the unconscious and a sign of schizophrenia. Subsequently, what he considered essential was not the presence of a particular content but the attitude towards it and the way in which this content could reach the individual's personal view of the world.

The case of Miss Miller evokes scenarios that are very close to Jung's problematic, of which *The Red Book*[24] in particular will later give a few elements. The theme of the hero, of course, but also the displacement of an erotic investment on a symbolic object, God in this case, will receive a considerable development in the Jungian works. Miss Miller's God is a pure product of transformation of an investment presented by Jung himself as sexual. What can we deduce from this? For Jung, the term "libido" is not devoid of sexual connotations, but at the same time he must discard any exclusively sexual definition of this notion. It is in fact this exclusively sexual aspect in Freud that raises questions since, for Jung, the sexual instinct is only one instinct among others. Jung refers to Cicero's definition of the libido as desire, which he then defines as being closer to that given by the Stoics: libido as unbridled greed. The term libido is for Jung equivalent to that of energy. Therefore, the libido is *more than* sexual drive, it is psychic energy. We have nothing against this definition, which does not exclude its sexual origin. But we still have to agree, and this is at the heart of the question, on the term "sexual". It is quite clear that Jung has a poor grasp of what is meant by sexual according to Freud and the correspondence does nothing to remedy this. For Jung, the withdrawal in schizophrenia is not a libidinal withdrawal, it is a withdrawal of vital interest. Jung does not understand how the withdrawal in schizophrenia is a libidinal withdrawal in so far as this withdrawal affects the function of the reality.[25] Jung cannot understand that the relationship to reality is governed by a sexual function and that means, in the Freudian sense, a gap from the biological function because of the connection between language and the body. It is quite clear that this difference remains alien to Jung. According to Freud, what makes the "sexual" different from the biological is perfectly illustrated by the example of sucking, taken from the *Three Essays*, something which was debated between them in the correspondence. The baby no longer sucks to eat, but sucks for pleasure, to reproduce the experience of satisfaction. This is where the gap lies. For Freud, the sexual is this gap and the libido is the energy that results from this gap. Nevertheless, Freud's use of the term "sexual" to designate the sphere of sexual relations maintains a certain ambiguity, hence the discussion about libido, sexual or not. Jung goes so far as to give the example of castrati, whose absence of libidinous interest in reality does not make them schizophrenic, hence his preference for the term psychic energy.

For Jung, symbols, as products of the transformation of the libido, are therefore not *exclusively* sexual but are nevertheless predominantly so. Symbols themselves lose all meaning when they do not have against them a force that can resist them. The strongest of these is sexuality, of which most symbols are more or less analogical representations. It is therefore the drive energy that lends its force to symbols with "most" symbols being sexual representations. Including, Jung continues, religious symbols. Jung also affirms that, if primitive Christianity distanced itself so much from instinctual life and in particular from sexuality by advocating asceticism, it is indeed because this sexuality is at its origin and its traces are visible in Christian symbolism. The Christian religion would not have succeeded so well in its process of metamorphosis of the libido if its archetypal analogies had not been so well adapted to the instinct that was to be modified. Jung thus situates Christianity, despite everything, as the inverted symbol of a sexuality that is too prevalent or too wild.

This is what the case of Miss Miller seeks to demonstrate. The religious metamorphosis has as its starting point a sexual demand which, in Miss Miller's case, cannot be fulfilled and remains for her in a fantasy state. For Jung, this religious metamorphosis constitutes a kind of indispensable stage that must be passed through, just like its "sacrificial" exit. Sacrifice, a deliberate renunciation of the maternal, must occur as a form of castration, after the phase of regression. It is the regression that will allow us to reach the universe of the archetypes, equivalent to the "symbolic father", and to elaborate, via the symbol, a rebirth, a true symbolic resurrection,[26] which does not leave aside the instinctual energy since it is included in the archetype. Jung confers a numinous feature to the archetype; archetypes are at the origin of the religious experiences from which rites are derived. The assimilation of symbols releases a certain amount of psychic energy, which can then be used on a conscious level, in an analogy with the rites of primitive men, which allow energy to be mobilised for specific purposes. It is interesting to note how close Jung's function of symbols is to that of the primitive men for whom the social group is just as predominant; we are reminded of what Lévi-Strauss says in the text *L'efficacité symbolique.*[27] *The Metamorphoses* were developed in the years 1909–1912. They were therefore contemporary and central to *The Freud–Jung Letters*[28] and became one of the ingredients of the two men rupture. The points of contradiction were first ignored and then, when recognised, they lead directly to the rupture. The *Letters* are disappointing in this respect, but nevertheless contain the elements of the dialogue that we want to reinstate.

The Freud–Jung letters

Jung's first visit to Freud took place on 3 March 1907. On his return to Zurich, Jung once again mentioned the reticence, even "emotional inhibitions", that the concept of libido caused in his entourage, particularly in Bleuler and in himself:

Is it not conceivable, in view of the limited conception of sexuality that prevails nowadays, that the sexual terminology should be reserved only for the most extreme forms of your "libido," and that a less offensive collective term should be established for all the libidinal manifestations?[29]

In April[30] and May[31] 1907, Freud communicated to Jung his ideas concerning projection in paranoia. For a representational content to be projected outwards, its libidinal investment must have been withdrawn beforehand. The libido leaves the object representation, which can then be treated as a perception and projected outwards. It was *the libidinal invest-ment that designated it as inner.*[32] This representational content then has the character of a perception which generates belief. The hostility towards the object is the endogenous perception of libidinal disinvestment. The object investment then returns to the ego, which is over-invested, hence the megalomania. The failure of the process means that the object, when sought out again, will be attached, after inversion into displeasure, to the per-ceptions that can be elevated to the level of hallucinations. The libidinal origin gives the delusion its strength.

In October 1907, in response to Freud who had reproached him for his laziness when it came to writing, Jung explained one of the reasons; he felt so much veneration for him:

... it is rather that my veneration for you has something of the character of a "religious" crush. Though it does not really bother me, I still feel it is disgusting and ridiculous because of its undeniable erotic undertone. This abominable feeling comes from the fact that as a boy I was the victim of a sexual assault by a man I once worshipped[33]. Even in Vienna the remarks of the ladies ("enfin seuls," etc.) sickened me, although the reason for it was not clear to me at the time. This feeling, which I still have not quite got rid of, hampers me considerably. Another manifestation of it is that I find psychological insight makes relations with colleagues who have a strong transference to me downright disgusting. I therefore fear your confidence. I also fear the same reaction from you when I speak of my intimate affairs.[34]

Jung associated these elements of his transference to Freud with a dream he had during his visit to Vienna:

... I dreamt that I saw you walking beside me as a very, very frail old man. Ever since then the dream has been preying on my mind, but to no purpose. The solution came (as usual) only after I had confessed my worries to you. The dream sets my mind at rest about your +++dangerousness [...] I don't know whether I am telling you anything new when I say that the history of Jensen's childhood is now clear to me. A very beautiful solution is to be found in the stories "The Red Umbrella" and "In the Gothic House."! Both, particularly the first, are wonderful parallels of Gradiva, sometimes down to the finest details. The problem is one of brother-sister love.[35]

Jung also develops his own ideas on paranoia.

The psychoses (the incurable ones) should probably be regarded as defensive encapsulations that have misfired, or rather, have been carried to extremes. The Fliess case bears this out [...] The hysteric, besides repressing reality, makes repeated attempts to link up with it again, the paranoiac forgoes even this and is only intent on keeping up his libido defences. Hence the fixation of the complexes [...] The paranoiac always seeks inner solutions, the hysteric outer ones. [36]

Freud approves of Jung's remarks, adding that he is the only one who can give a little of himself! He then returns to paranoia. In this case, the reality test is evaded, because what comes from outside does not need it. Paranoia corresponds to a failed detachment of libido, since it returns in the projection, and the intensity of the investment changes into certainty.[37]

In April 1908, the first Freudian psychology congress took place in Salzburg, during which the first analytical periodical, the Jarhbuch, was founded and Jung was to be its editor in chief. Jung published a paper on dementia praecox. According to Jung, dementia praecox was the result of a fixation at an extremely early stage when the sexual complex is still entirely auto-erotic. Freud replied,

It seems doubtful to me that the precocity of the infantile fixation creates the predisposition to Dem. pr.; the matter calls for thorough investigation.[38]

And later on:

One thing and another have turned my thoughts to mythology and I am beginning to suspect that myth and neurosis have a common core.[39]

In the first issue of the Jahrbuch, Jung's article entitled *The importance of the father for the destiny of the individual* would appear, while Jung himself became the father of a boy at the same time. He wrote to Freud:

My paper on the father complex is no great shakes but is, I think, a decent job. I hope you will like it. In any event its staunchness to the cause leaves nothing to be desired.[40]

This, however, is the least that can be said. Jung, in fact, asserted:

Freud has repeatedly stated with unmistakable clarity that the psycho-sexual relationship of the child with his parents, especially with the father, is of decisive importance for the content of a later neurosis. Indeed, the relationship with the parents is the infantile channel par excellence through which the libido of later life flows back when it encounters obstacles, thus reviving long-forgotten childhood dreams.[41]

This was followed by a series of clinical cases in support of this assertion. But we also find, at the end of the article, the premise of what will be his later elaboration, namely, the link with history and, more particularly, the history of religions: the *pater familias*, elevated to the rank of Jehovah by the religion of the Old Testament, inspires this same fear that the father aroused, from which only the prophets were able to free themselves. For the individual, the father is replaced by a pair of opposites—God and the Devil—both, respectively, symbols of repression and sexual pleasure, whose opposition is accentuated in neurosis. God is thus at this time, as seen later in the *Metamorphoses*, linked to repression.

In March 1909, Jung left his post at the Burghölzli. At the end of March, he made a second visit to Vienna. On his return to Zurich, he wrote to Freud. In connection to a patient who was of great concern to him, he put forward the idea that if there is psychoanalysis, *there must also be psychosynthesis, which creates the future according to the same laws.* Following the visit to Freud, he himself had a "great dream", the analysis of which he had just completed.[42] This was the year of the trip to America. Jung was invited to Clark University to give a series of lectures on the association test experiment. Freud had already received an invitation, independently. They decided to make the trip together in August 1909, accompanied by Ferenczi. Jung had become increasingly interested in mythology and the history of symbols. He saw in this a source that would make it possible to find the phylogenesis of neuroses:

> We shall not solve the background of neurosis and psychosis without mythology and the history of civilisations; this has become quite clear to me; *comparative anatomy* goes with *embryology*, and without the latter, the latter is a game of nature misunderstood in its depths.[43]

His aim, as he expressed it in a conference held in January in Herisau, which would serve as a matrix for *Metamorphoses of the Libido and its Symbols*, is: "To found the 'symbolic' in developmental psychology, that is, to show that the *primum movens* of individual fantasy is individual conflict, but that the matter (or form, as one prefers), is mythical, or mythologically typical".[44] Freud shared his enthusiasm. He replied:

> Your deepened view of symbolism has all my sympathy [...] True, what you write about it now is only a hint, but in a direction where I too am searching, namely, archaic regression, which I hope to master through mythology and the development of language.[45]

But, for Freud, the understanding of myth is impossible without the theory of infantile sexuality.[46] Jung again refers to what he had said in the Herisau lecture:

The first thing about your conception of the ucs. is that it is in striking agreement with what I said in my January lecture on symbolism. I explained there, that "logical" thinking is thinking in words, which like discourse is directed outwards, "Analogical" or fantasy thinking is emotionally toned, pictorial and wordless, not discourse but an inner-directed rumination on materials belonging to the past. Logical thinking is "verbal thinking." Analogical thinking is archaic, unconscious, not put into words and hardly formulable in words.[47]

In the meantime, Freud was busy writing his essay, *A Childhood Memory of Leonardo da Vinci*. Jung was thrilled. For him, the transition to the mythological emerged from this writing with an internal necessity. In March 1910, the second Congress took place in Nuremberg, during which the International Psychoanalytical Association was founded, with Jung as president. In June 1910, Jung sent the text of the Herisau lecture[48] to Freud, who received it with mixed feelings. According to him, the essay shed more light on the mythological than on the symbolic,[49] for Freud of infantile origin, being therefore ontogenetic.[50] During this period, Freud worked on the Schreber case that Jung had pointed out to him. The *Letters* are peppered with "Schreberian" expressions by both of them. Jung himself made various allusions to the Schreber case in *Psychology of Dementia praecox* and the *Metamorphoses*. In *President Schreber*,[51] Freud made a series of interpretations in a manner that could be said to be the reverse of Jung's, reducing a series of symbols to their origin, which, in this case, according to him was the Schreber family. He thus proceeded to a true translation of Schreber's "basic language", as Freud called Schreber's language:

First the father complex: obviously Flechsig-father-God-sun form a series. The "middle" Flechsig points to a brother who like the father was already "blessed," that is, dead, at the time of the illness. The forecourts of heaven or "anterior realms of God" (breasts!) are the women of the family, the "posterior realms of God" (buttocks!) are the father and his sublimation, God [...] The castration complex is only too evident. Don't forget that Schreber's father was a doctor. As such, he performed miracles, he miracled. In other words, the delightful characterization of God-that he knows how to deal only with corpses and has no idea of living people-and the absurd miracles that are performed on him are a bitter satire on his father's medical art.[52]

These equivalences will be developed by Freud in *President Schreber*.[53] Here, we are at the heart of the matter: the Schreberian language, the "basic" language, speaks in symbols. For Freud, these symbols constitute metaphors for the different elements of the castration complex, notably Schreber's relationship with his father, of which the figure of God would constitute the sublimation. Of course, and this is the whole point, these metaphors are in no way considered as such by Schreber.

In March 1911, Freud asked Jung directly about the question of symbols:

> Can you do anything with this formula: the symbol is an ucs. substitute for a cs. concept; symbol formation is the initial stage of concept formation, just as repression is the forerunner of judgment?[54]

Jung's response:

> The definition of symbol fits if regarded from the purely intellectual standpoint. But what if a symbol is put in the place of a clear concept in order to repress it? To take an example: in answer to the question, How was the first man created? "An American Indian myth says: from the hilt of a sword and a shuttle". Here symbol formation seems to be aiming at something quite different from concept formation. Symbol formation, it seems to me, is the necessary bridge to the rethinking of long familiar concepts from which the libidinal cathexis is partly withdrawn by canalizing it into a series of intellectual parallels (mythological theories).[55]

In September 1911, the Weimar Congress took place. Freud's contribution was a supplement to the analysis of Schreber with the following commentary:

> This little supplement ... undoubtedly shows the validity of Jung's propositions, namely that the mythopoeic forces of humanity are not extinct, but still produce in neuroses the same psychic products as in the earliest times.[56]

Freud quoted Jung several times in *President Schreber*. He paid tribute to his work on dementia praecox, in particular his recognition of the traces of former object investments in the delusion. He also endorsed Jung's comment about the successive divisions of God and Fleschig as being mechanisms to diminish the power of all-powerful figures. Jung returned to Schreber in a letter the following November:

> That passage in your Schreber analysis where you ran into the libido problem (loss of libido = loss of reality) is one of the points where our mental paths cross. In my view the concept of libido as set forth in the *Three Essays* needs to be supplemented by the genetic factor to make it applicable to Dem. praec.[57]

Freud's response:

> I should be very much interested in knowing what you mean by an extension of the concept of the libido to make it applicable to Dem. pr. I

am afraid there is a misunderstanding between us, the same sort of thing as when you once said in an article that to my way of thinking libido is identical with any kind of desire, whereas in reality I hold very simply that there are two basic drives and that only the power behind the sexual drive can be termed libido.[58]

Jung's response:

The loss of the reality function in Dem. pr. cannot be reduced to repression of libido (defined as sexual hunger). Not by me, at any rate. Your doubt shows me that in your eyes as well the problem cannot be solved in this way [...] The essential point is that I try to replace the descriptive concept of libido by a genetic one. Such a concept covers not only the recent sexual libido but all those forms of it which have long since split off into organized activities. A wee bit of biology was unavoidable here.[59]

The points of disagreement were thus laid down but the relationship remained cordial. For Jung, independence of spirit is a priority. He explained this by quoting Nietzche's *Zarathustra*, one of his favourite works:

One repays a teacher badly if one remains only a pupil [...] You had not yet sought yourselves when you found me. Thus do all believers. Now I bid you lose me and find yourselves; and only when you have all denied me will I return to you.[60]

The exchange between Freud and Jung then shifts to another subject and focuses on the question of incest. Meanwhile, Freud's elaboration of *Totem and Taboo* was beginning to take shape. The murder of the tyrant father, perpetrated by the brothers with the aim of taking his wives, is followed by the cannibalistic meal that achieves identification by absorption of his body. But since this inaugural murder can only give rise to fratricidal struggles, the renunciation of what had motivated the murder itself follows in the form of the institution of the prohibition of incest and the law of exogamy. It should be noted that this second stage is often neglected. The murder of the father solves nothing, only the renunciation and the establishment of the law are effective. The place of renunciation is in line with Jungian thought. On the other hand, the prohibition of totemic murder, which is religious in nature, becomes the prohibition of fratricidal, social murder, while the resentment against the father that led to the murder is extinguished to make way for a love of the father, the other branch of the initial ambivalence, which is itself at the foundation of religion. The two commandments of totemism, the two taboo prescriptions that form its core, coincide with the two Oedipal crimes. The totem is designated as an ancestor; the identification of man with his totem constitutes the very essence of totemism. The relationship of primitive men to the totem is found in the child's attitude towards animals, which is the origin of infantile phobias. For Jung, the incest ban is essentially a symbol:

> From this standpoint we must say that incest is forbidden not because it is desired but because the free-floating anxiety regressively reactivates infantile material and turns it into a ceremony of atonement (as though incest had been, or might have been, desired) [...] The aetiological significance of the incest prohibition must be compared directly with the so-called sexual trauma, which usually owes its aetiological role only to regressive reactivation.[61]

Jung therefore emphasised regression on the one hand, and on the other, drew a parallel between the prohibition of incest and sexual trauma. He did this to underline its symbolic value, rather than a real one, something to which Freud is sensitive, hence his response:

> I value your letter for the warning it contains, and the reminder of my first big error, when I mistook fantasies for realities. I shall be careful and keep my eyes open every step of the way.[62]

Jung returned to the issue a little later:

> The salient fact is simply the regressive movement of libido and not the mother, otherwise people without parents would have no chance to develop an incest complex; whereas I know from experience that the contrary is true. In certain circumstances, indeed as a general rule, the fantasy object is called "mother".[63]

In May 1912, the Kreuzlingen gesture occurred marking the beginning of the period of gradual rupture between Freud and Jung that would last until 1915. Freud went to Lake Constance in Kreuzlingen, very close to Jung's home, to visit the ailing Binswanger, without informing Jung. He explained this in his letter of 13 June, citing a lack of time. During the summer and autumn of 1912, Jung travelled to America for a series of lectures during which he exposed some of his divergences from Freudian theory. On his return, he wrote to Freud:

> Naturally I also made room for those of my views which deviate in places from the hitherto existing conceptions, particularly in regard to the libido theory. I found that my version won over many people who until now had been put off by the problem of sexuality in neurosis.[64]

Freud would respond much later in *Contribution to the History of the Analytical Movement*:

The modification introduced by Jung broke the links between the phenomena and the instinctive life [...] Morality and religion must not be sexualised, both being originally something "superior"[65] [...] It was the desire to eliminate what is shocking in the family complexes, so as not to find these shocking elements in religion and morality, which dictated to Jung all the modifications he made to psychoanalysis.[66]

The Munich conference took place on 24 November 1912. Freud and Jung discussed the Kreuzlingen gesture and a pseudo-reconciliation ensued. At the end of the lunch, Freud fainted. On the 29th, he wrote to Jung about the *Metamorphoses*, the second part of which had just been published:

I am gradually coming to terms with this paper (yours, I mean) and I now believe that in it you have brought us a great revelation, though not the one you intended. You seem to have solved the riddle of all mysticism, showing it to be based on the symbolic utilization of complexes that have outlived their function.[67]

Jung took these last words very badly and retorted by underlining Freud's neurosis, bringing up Freud's statement during their stay together in America that he could not confide without losing his authority, a statement that he had augured well for the future. The relationship then deteriorated. Jung reproached Freud for being an authoritarian father who kept his sons in submission. On 3 January 1913, Freud proposed to Jung that they break off their private relationship.[68]

In July, Jung wrote to Freud about the article "A Dream as Evidence" and hoped to clear up what he considered to be misunderstandings raised by the article:

A second misunderstanding seems to be that you think we deny the wish-fulfilment theory of dreams. We fully admit the soundness of the wish-fulfilment theory, but we maintain that this way of interpreting dreams touches only the surface, that it stops at the symbol, and that further interpretation is possible. When, for instance, a coitus wish appears in a dream, this wish can be analysed further, since this archaic expression with its tiresome monotony of meaning needs retranslating into another medium. We recognize the soundness of the wish-fulfilment theory up to a certain point, but we go beyond it. In our view it does not exhaust the meaning of the dream.[69]

The Munich Congress on the function of dreams was held in September 1913. During the re-election of the President of the International Association, 52 of the members present abstained to avoid a unanimous re-election of Jung.

The break

In October, Jung wrote to Freud that he had learned from Maeder that Freud doubted his *bona fides*. Jung then resigned from the Jahrbuch.[70] Shortly afterwards, Jung went to Schaffhausen to pick up his wife Emma and the children. On the train to Schaffhausen, he was overcome by visions of floods overrunning Switzerland.[71] In April 1914, he resigned as president of the International Psychoanalytical Association. Jung's last letter to Freud was written in 1923. Jung referred a patient to him, a Jew who did not want to admit his Judaism.

Narcissism

Freud published two articles in the first volume of the Jahrbuch of 1914 and it could be considered that he continued his debate with Jung here. In *On the History of the Psychoanalytic Movement*,[72] Freud intended to show how the theories of those he called his opponents, who were at the same time considered to be analysands hence a certain ambiguity that is not lost on him, could not enter the field of what he believed should be called psychoanalysis. Any orientation that was connected to transference and resistance had the right to call itself psychoanalysis, even if it led to different results. Freud paid tribute to Jung's work, as well as that of Bleuler and the Zurich school for their contribution to the study of schizophrenia, yet he remained firm in his position on the points he considered crucial for psychoanalysis, in particular the importance of regression. *Analysis, for Freud, is incapable of elucidating the present without bringing it back to the past.* We know that on this point, Jung will develop a different way of thinking, although also based on regression.[73]

A certain confusion in Jungian thought is noted by Freud. We can say, having confronted it throughout this work, that Jungian thought is diffuse. In order to understand it, it is necessary to cross-check the different parts of the works; it has not the implacable rigour of Freud. Freud's critique also reviewed various specific points. The libidinal charge must be removed from the complexes rather than be turned away and pushed towards sublimation. The rupture of the links between the phenomena and the instinctive life is the problematic point of the Jungian elaboration, indeed it is a point that is foreclosed. Freud continued to elaborate on this with *Narcissism: an introduction.* Here, narcissism[74] is conceived as the libidinal complement to the egoism of the drive of self-preservation. The original libidinal investment of the ego, a part of which will later be ceded to the objects, can also be withdrawn from the objects. It was only with the notion of *the object investment* that it became possible to distinguish a sexual energy, the libido, from the energy of the drive of the ego. This bipartition, the relevance of which Freud nevertheless questioned, was imposed on him by the analysis of transference neuroses. But in schizophrenic patients (contrary to neurotics), the libido is withdrawn from people and things of the external world to be brought to the ego, so that this attitude which can be qualified as narcissism appears as a secondary state built on the basis of a primary narcissism. For Freud, the libido becomes free through frustration. Let us insist on this term. It is a frustration (*Versagung*), *the refusal of satisfaction of a drive claim*, which allows the libido to detach from objects and withdraw into the ego. But let us ask the question: is this libido, detached from the object and returned to the ego, still of a sexual nature?

Freud also made a point of differentiating between sublimation and idealisation, a differentiation that is essential for our purpose. The process of sublimation concerns the object libido and relates to the drive which then chooses a goal other than the sexual goal. Idealisation is a process that concerns the object, which is "psychically enlarged and exalted without its nature being changed". It is a substitute for the initial narcissism. It is to this Ego-ideal that love formerly destined for the real ego is addressed. But the idealisation can concern the domain of the ego libido as well as that of the object libido. The Ego-ideal[75] is thus the result of the displacement of the initial narcissism. It is the projected substitute of narcissism in the form of an ideal. The formation of the ideal, increasing the demands on the ego, goes in the direction of repression, whereas sublimation provides another way out by saving the repression. Here again the place of the object is central in this differentiation. The establishment of an ideal in place of narcissism, Freud tells us, does not imply the sublimation of the drive. The Ego-ideal, in a way, requires this sublimation but it is incapable of producing it. On the contrary, the critical instance of observation unceasingly measures the gap between the ego and its ideal. The neurotic who, because of his excessive object investments, is impoverished in his ego, is unable to accomplish his Ego-ideal. He then falls back on an object endowed with qualities that he cannot attain. This is how an object choice marked by the seal of the symptom is constructed.

From this text on narcissism, it is easier to understand how the gap between Freud and Jung widens. Finally, superimposed on this gap is, on the one hand, idealisation with its corollary of repression and censorship and, on the other, sublimation, the path to freedom, so to speak. This gap will continue right up to the question of dreams, on which Freud always pulls to the side of censorship, whereas Jung, who does not know this word, focuses on its progressive feature: weaving the thread of displacement which is the path to sublimation. Freud needs to thwart the obstacles of censorship, whereas Jung jumps over them to directly catch the thread of sublimation. The formation of the Ego-ideal and its connection to the "father", the sublimation that does without it, constitutes the crossroads where their paths intersect and diverge. This divergence continues on the role of the symbol, a sign of repression, as something to be deciphered for Freud, but to be constructed for Jung, for whom collective symbolism is the only available path for connection. Freud thinks in terms of repression and neurosis whereas Jung thinks in terms of symbols and psychosis.

Symbols have been at the heart of Jungian thought since *Psychology of Dementia praecox* and the association tests. Jung focused on the formation of symbols since his field, at the time, was one where symbols are most obviously lacking. Symbols are, first of all, considered as the instrument suitable to compensate for the failure of associations. Their function is associative. In this sense, the production of symbols in dementia praecox is an attempt to repair a symbolic defect. This is in line with the idea of delusion as an attempt at healing. Nevertheless, this attempt is only partially successful because the subject's mooring to the symbol is still missing. The seamstress does not identify with Socrates, she is Socrates. Later on, the *Metamorphoses* highlighted the displacement of the libido onto a symbolic object that has become a kind of substitute and a metamorphosis of the libido. The vector of symbolisation is the comparison, the support of a total or partial identification with a trait from the instinctual life, direct or displaced. In any case, symbols are a way of speaking *that short-circuits the vagaries of singularity.*

Sabina Spielrein: between Freud and Jung

A certain number of these points of rupture reappeared under the pen of Sabina Spielrein, whose particular place between Freud and Jung is well known. But Spielrein, like ourselves no doubt, wondered about the transferential part of the gap that separated them and contributed her stone to the construction of a bridge, a Jungian motif par excellence, between their two thoughts. In *Destruction as the cause of coming into being*, prefiguring the Freudian elaboration of the death drive, she asks the question: how can the procreative instinct give rise to negative effects alongside the positive effects we expect, among which are anguish and disgust? She evokes the work of Jung, in particular several passages from the *Metamorphoses*:

> Passionate longing, i.e. the libido, has two aspects: it is the power which beautifies everything, and in certain cases, destroys everything [...] To be fruitful provokes one's downfall; at the rise of the next generation, the previous one has exceeded its peak: our descendants become our most dangerous enemies, for whom we are unprepared. They will survive and take the power out of our enfeebled hands [...] Whoever relinquishes experiencing a risky undertaking must stifle an erotic wish, committing a form of self-murder. This explains that the death fantasies often accompany the renunciation of the erotic wish.[76]

Thus, Spielrein continues, there is something deep within the individual that drives him to harm himself and to take pleasure in it. Such a desire for suffering would be incomprehensible if we were to consider only the ego which, in fact, pursues only its own pleasure.

In patients with Dementia praecox who transform ego-images into objective or collective representations, inadequate affect, indifference, appears. This decreases when we succeed in establishing a relationship to the ego. For example a patient said: "the earth became dirtied by urine" instead of "I became dirtied by the sexual act". Therein lies my concept of symbolic expression. The symbol is an analogous to the painful image, but it is less differentiated than an ego-image.[77]

For Spielrein, it is indeed the recourse to symbols, in *place of the I*, that suppresses the place of the affect. The subjectivisation of symbols restores it. Here, Spielrein attempts an articulation between what can be considered as the outline of a conception of the death drive and the question of symbols by integrating the place of the affect. Another very interesting idea extends the Jungian conception of symbols while formulating it in more explicit terms. In dementia praecox, there is a sort of *collectivisation of experience*, to the detriment of the ego, which reacts by displacing the affect.

Freud believes that dementia praecox behaves as if there were withdrawal or regression of libido, followed by a struggle between the withdrawal of the libido and its distribution. I interpret the illness as a battle between the two antagonistic tendencies of the collective and the personal psyches. The collective psyche wants to make the ego-image into an impersonal, typical image. The personal psyche tries to restrain this dissolution, causing patients anxiously to transfer the feeling-tone of dissolving complexes to collateral associations that the ego then fixes (inadequate affect).[78]

Individual representations are assimilated into archaic, cultural representations, i.e. *individual representations are dissolved and transformed into typical representations* common to the whole species. Spielrein emphasises the analogy between what happens in dementia praecox and what happens in art, where a transformative impulse dissolves individual representational contents into a similar, typical, species-specific material whose outward projection constitutes it as art.

Every content appearing in consciousness is a product that differentiates from other, psychologically older, contents [...] If we want to make our specific content accessible to others, we must de-differentiate it: we clothe the specifically personal content and stamp it with the symbolic form of the applicable collective type. Here we use our second tendency to assimilate or dissolve which opposes differentiation. Assimilation produces the shaping of a unit, considered to be an "I" into one considered to be a "We".[79]

This work of assimilation, transforming individual content into collective content subsequently, opens the door to identification. It is through identification with the work of art that the individual, to a certain extent, will turn this collective content back into an individual content.[80] A symbol ceases to be a symbol at the very moment when we recognise in it our own disposition. A trait is recognised as ours from its presentation in, and belonging to, a symbol. This is what Jung does in his method of dream interpretation, as we shall see later. This is also what is at stake in the treatment of psychoses, that is to say, recognising a personal trait in its collective, symbolic representation.

Spielrein, in her correspondence with Jung, pointed out everything that separated him from Freud. For her, the gap in their concepts was forged by reasons of another order than that of a theoretical divergence. She gave several examples, in particular the function of the symptom. In her opinion, where Jung sees neurosis as a process of regression, Freud sees it as an arrest of development. When Jung says that the unfulfilment of a goal of existence leads to neurosis, i.e. to regression, Freud, on the other hand, says that as a result of a developmental arrest, one can no longer find a goal in existence, i.e. one can no longer sufficiently carry out sublimation. There is no contradiction. However, she thinks that, if Freud will probably never understand Jung's innovations, Jung, on the other hand, would be able to understand Freud very well if a personal affective position did not prevent him from doing so.[81]

After his separation from Freud, Jung continued his research on symbols (but independently from the question of psychosis) through two main avenues: the study of dreams and the development of the concept of archetype.

The symbol, an articulation between the individual and the group

This interest in the study of myths was shared by Freud and Jung, as we have seen, but also, in the same years, by the analysts around them. Rank published *The Myth of the Birth of the Hero* in 1909, a text on which Freud would later build in *Moses and Monotheism*. *Dreams and Myths*, by Abraham, was also published the same year. Freud's typical dreams are its starting point. Typical dreams are characterised by the presence of "fixed" symbols, for which *the association regularly fails.*[82] These dreams are individual but contain desires that are shared by all people. These same desires are at the basis of myths and this is the point on which Jung built in his elaboration of the archetype. For him, dreams and their spontaneous presentation of symbols are the main sources of knowledge of symbolism. But another source also exists, a collective one, constituted by religious imagery, which come from dreams and creative imagination. In dreams, therefore, individual elements drawn from the personal experience of the dreamer coexist with unknown elements. The question arises, however, of why these unknown elements can't be linked to his experience. These elements, which cannot be described as individuals and cannot be drawn from the dreamer's experience, are what Freud, for his part, as we shall see later, calls "archaic residues". These elements seem to be innate and constitute the heritage of the human spirit. Jung connected these archaic residues to the "archetypes". The archetype lies in an "instinctive" tendency to represent patterns; their representation can vary considerably in detail without losing its fundamental pattern. Archetypes function as complexes; they are both *images and emotions*, and we can only speak of archetypes when both aspects are present simultaneously. When charged with affectivity, the images acquire numinosity,[83] in other words psychic energy. They become dynamic and this necessarily leads to consequences. Let us translate: the archetype is connected to the instinctual life—and its *figurative potentiality*—whose energy is described by Jung through the term numinous. The numinous is the name of the Jungian energetics, but an energetics that sets aside partial drives. The archetype consists of representative potentiality rather than representation, that is, what we retain. However, it must be acknowledged that Jungian formulations often maintain a confusion between these two terms.

Jung's archetype: a collective unconscious

In his interview with Jung for *Combat*, Mircea Eliade[84] referred to the Jungian elaboration on archetypes as an immense reservoir of "historical memories"—a collective memory—where the history of all humanity survives in its essence. Eliade indicated that it was indeed as a result of his own dreams, and as early as 1909, that Jung was led to suppose the existence of a collective unconscious.

But the collective unconscious also found anthropological support in Jung's study of the psychology of primitive people. Among them, there was a prejudice of identity of the psychological structure of humans, which is not, moreover, the prerogative of primitive people, but among the latter, this identity is also found between man and nature. Animals, plants, but also rivers and mountains are endowed with a human psychology. This prejudice, when perpetuated, is clearly a powerful survival of a primitive state of mind which is based on an *insufficient differentiation of individual consciousness*. Primitiveness possesses a diffuse consciousness of the universe combined with a total unconsciousness of the subject submitted to representations.[85] Individual consciousness differentiated from the consciousness of others is, therefore, a "recent" acquisition. For Jung, it is only an island emerging in the ocean of the collective unconscious, always ready to submerge it:

We have now found the object which the libido chooses when it is freed from the personal, *infantile form of transference*[86]. It follows its own gradient down into the depths of the unconscious, and there activates what has lain slumbering from the beginning [...] We mentioned earlier that the unconscious contains, as it were, two layers: the personal and the collective. The personal layer ends at the earliest memories of infancy, but the collective layer comprises the preinfantile period, that is, the residues of ancestral life. Whereas the memory-images of the personal unconscious are, as it were, filled out, because they are images personally experienced by the individual, the archetypes of the collective unconscious are not filled out because they are forms not personally experienced. When, on the other hand, psychic energy regresses, going beyond even the period of early infancy, and breaks into the legacy of ancestral life, the mythological images are awakened: these are the archetypes.[87]

Magical or demonic influences: such attributes indicate that the collective unconscious is projected. Most of the archetypes appear in the form of *projections*, and they settle wherever a motive (which Jung calls contingent) invites them to.[88] But how can we avoid the permanent dissociation, or the constant rift, between the individual and collective psyche? This is why individuation cannot do without symbols as the primitive expression of the unconscious and a means of expression of the collective unconscious data, but also a means of preserving the unity of consciousness when faced with the process of disintegration caused by the unconscious. This is where the role of symbols lies—through and beyond religious belief—which, thanks to symbolism, allows the primitive man in us to express himself.

The concept of the archetype is also accompanied by energetics. The awareness resulting from the confrontation of the collective unconscious and the individual psyche also allows the latter to recover the energy invested in the deeper layers of the unconscious. Archetypes are therefore dynamic at the same time. Because of its location in the collective transpersonal layer of the unconscious, the libido attached to the archetypes can function as a transformer of psychic energy. In the unconscious, the continuous work of the archetypes produces processes similar to the formation of myths.

> Such a continuity can only exist if we assume a certain unconscious condition as an inherited a priori factor. By this I naturally do not mean the inheritance of ideas, which would be difficult if not impossible to prove. I suppose, rather, the inherited quality to be something like the formal possibility of producing the same or similar ideas over and over again. I have called this possibility the "archetype".[89]

The archetype is therefore psychoid: it is *potentially, conditionally, psychic*. The archetype is what gives a form to the drive energy. It consists of the unconscious property inherited from previous generations, to be conceived as a formal possibility of reproducing similar or, at least, analogous ideas. This possibility is what Jung calls an archetype. This is an important point; it is a matrix, a symbolic matrix, or rather a matrix of the symbolic, which, when put into action, will manifest itself as a psychic representation. It is this potentiality to become psychic that, for us, gives to the archetype its value as a trace. This trace, actualised and "written", becomes psychic.[90]

According to Jung, the unconscious, therefore, produces historical and not only personal contents. This is a mythological type of material and is the residue of a lack of differentiation between individual consciousness and primitive group consciousness. The Freudian unconscious seemed to him to include only the remains of consciousness, like a warehouse where everything that consciousness had rejected was piled up and abandoned, whereas for Jung, the unconscious constitutes this matrix capable of autonomous acts. The contents of the collective unconscious withdraw by themselves. They had not been repressed but, on the contrary, they have autonomy.[91] This divergence is a difference in the emphasis placed on one or other of the properties of the unconscious and is caricatured by Jung. It is both topical and dynamic. It is made up of two points: the question of the unconscious, as repressed or not, and the dynamics of the unconscious. For Jung, only the personal unconscious is repressed, while the collective unconscious, the residue within which the subject is not differentiated, has never reached consciousness. In this way it comes closer to the Freudian concept of primal repression.

For Jung, the collective unconscious is thus *a residue that relates to an undifferentiation from the Other.* It is an undifferentiated material, made of traces, to be differentiated and engraved. *Without this inscription, it remains doomed to projection,* and this is perhaps the most interesting contribution, which comes directly from the work with psychosis but which goes far beyond it, since psychosis is not the exclusive domain of projection. The "writing" of this material is what allows its translation in terms of personal unconscious. The writing of these traces is the aim of the individuation process as a successive production of symbols, mainly in dreams but also, for Jung, through visions and other images, which he calls active imagination, under the impulse of transference. *Under transference, these traces are written in symbols.* This unconscious is therefore eminently dynamic. Of course, Jung neglects the dynamic aspect of the Freudian unconscious. Without this aspect, there would be no possible cure. Nevertheless, we think that Jung's conception, which proceeds directly from his apprehension of psychosis, highlights and sheds light on the articulation of the individual to the collective, which is covered by the term "individuation process".

It is during the individuation process and through the work of dreams (during an analysis), which plays a major role in this process. The unconscious produces a category of symbols that Jung calls mandalas, and which have the function of a reconciliation of opposites, of a mediation. The centre of a mandala is empty or occupied by a motif, but never by a divinity. The place of the divinity is to be taken by the totality of man, the Self.[92] The experience of the mandala is for Jung typical of those who cannot continue to project a divine image. But as a result of the withdrawal of projection and the introjection of this image, they are faced with a real danger of inflation and dissolution of their personality, as well as a danger of identification with the unconscious, which Jung calls ordinary madness.[93] The mandala is the representation and at the same time the support of an exclusive concentration on the centre, also known as the Self. It is a concentration on oneself and a limitation to oneself in order to avoid inflation and dissociation. This is how the search for this point of balance between the conscious and the unconscious, a sort of virtual point that Jung calls the Self, becomes necessary. This translation from the Ego to the Self results in the abolition of *mystical participation,* which amounts to making room for the reception of the unconscious. This term of mystical participation is borrowed from Lévy-Bruhl, who thus characterises what, in primitive mentality, has to do with *a remnant of a lack of differentiation between the subject and the object.*

> With a stroke of genius, Lévi-Bruhl had laid down the condition he calls participation mystique as the hall-mark of primitive mentality. As described by him, it is simply the indefinitely large remnant of the non-differentiation between subject and object [...] The unconscious is indeed projected into the object, and the object introjected into the subject, that is to say, made part of the subject's psychology. Plants and animals behave like humans; men are at the same time themselves and animals also, and everything is alive with spectres and gods. The civilised man naturally regards himself to be immeasurably above all this. Nonetheless, he is often identified with his parents for his whole life; or he is identified with his affects and shamelessly accuses others for the things he will not see in himself. He, too, in a word, has still a remnant of primal unconsciousness, that is to say, or the state of non-differentiation between subject and object.[94]

For Jung, it is true, the elaboration of archetypal traces is rendered in terms of access to consciousness and is also reduced to this access. The archetype accesses the conscious via the symbol, but *to the detriment of the singular traces of the object relation that preside over the choice of this symbol.* The role of God, for this pastor's son, is obviously exemplary of this avoidance, but Jung will return to it later to acknowledge his debt, as his dreams will testify.[95] The place of God in Jungian thought cannot be separated from his personal history but it cannot be reduced to it either. The category of the divine brings together the movements of projection, introjection and symbolisation and the related energetics. Nevertheless, in our opinion, the connections between the personal and the collective unconscious are not specified enough and the personal unconscious, which is not denied, is given too small a part. The identification with a trait of collective symbolism, testifying to a direct or displaced pulsional stake, is only retained. But this stake is kept at a distance from the signifying milestones of a personal history.

God: matrix of the archetype

God, therefore, has a prominent place; he is the archetype par excellence. *The Red Book* is the fruit of the elaboration of the crisis Jung went through after his break with Freud.[96] It allows us to better grasp the foundations of Jungian thinking and the role attributed to religion in man. *The Red Book*, written by Jung during and after this crisis, presents the outline of what will become the individuation process. It is about the transformation of the link between Jung and the figure of God through a whole series of identifications and separations mediated by dreams and the "visions" that run through Jung at this time. But *The Red Book* is also the story of a loss suffered by God and by Jung at the same time. God loses his absolute character and becomes relative. We witness the birth of a new God marked by the seal of lacking. This operation, divine castration, is what supports the unconscious.

If the Self, the Jungian word for this conscious-unconscious whole, transits but only transits through God, it will be necessary, at the end of the process, to extract one's Self from God who could otherwise drag the Self into the unlimited. One will have to refuse the fusion and to recognise and respect a limit. It is this process of disengagement from God, occurring after a stage of necessary identification, lived in the mode of a true Passion, which will subsequently return in the Jungian concept of psychology and religion. Between theism and atheism, Jung proposes a new path: that of the relativity of the divine. But, as Christine Maillard says,[97] *The Red Book* is also to be understood as a re-reading of the history of Christianity conceived as a stage in the history of religions which makes Gnosticism, the constant reference of *The Red Book*, a compensatory current to Christianity, integrating repressed representations. In fact, if the life of Christ is to a high degree archetypal, it also represents the very life of the archetype. The question of the death of God is expressed there. Christ himself is this very type of the dead and metamorphosed God. Christ dies and is reborn restoring a new order and a transformed value that is to be recognised.

> This process is a lived, typical experience, that is, one that is frequently renewed, and that is why it is expressed in this place in the Christian mystery. This death, this loss, must be repeated and reproduced again and again: Christ always dies, just as he is always reborn; for the life of the archetype is timeless in comparison with our individual conditioning of time. [...] The myth says: he will not be found again where his body was deposited. The "body" is the outward and visible form, the past and present, but temporary and transient version of the supreme value. The myth, continuing its course, tells us that this value is reborn again in a miraculous but transformed way.[98]

But the death of God or his disappearance does not only refer to a Christian symbolism; it can be found in other religious universes which indicates for Jung their value as a *typical psychic process*.

God's death, or his disappearance, is by no means only a Christian symbol. The search which follows his death can still be seen today after the death of a Dalai Lama, and in antiquity it was celebrated in the annual search for the Kore. Such a wide distribution argues in favour of the universal occurrence of this typical psychic process: the highest value, which gives life and meaning, has got lost. This is a typical experience that has been repeated many times and its expression, therefore, occupies a central place in the Christian mystery.[99]

For Jung, then, Christian myth is only one of the possible actualisations of a transcendent universal destined to disappear and be reborn in another form, one of those psychic products called archetype, the archetype par excellence. From commonalities seen across the world, the myths could claim a universal form. The Christian universal aims at eliminating all differences and making a Unity prevail in their place—the ultimate Unity—which Christ symbolises. This is why the universal needs to be proclaimed again and again, because it is always in danger of being stripped of its unity by what is different. From the beginning of Christianity, several attempts have been made in this direction. The different forms of gnosis to which Jung refers have in common that they postulate two instances where it was claimed that there was only one.[100] There were two instances (or even several) because this new God—symbol of symbols, and emblematic of the function of the symbol—is also the product of the conciliation of opposites.

The conciliation of opposites, of which the symbol is the fruit, is introduced in *The Red Book* through the notion of Pleroma that Jung, in *The Seven Sermons to the Dead*,[101] borrows from Gnostic systems. The Jungian concept of Pleroma is said to be partly derived from that of Basilides of Alexandria, but also from that of Valentin.[102] Yet it is the character of Philemon, based on Ovid's *Metamorphoses*, who replaces Basilides in addressing the dead. The Pleroma, or fullness, is infinite, eternal and whole. It is undivided. *It is made up of all the qualities that constitute the divine world*, but it has no qualities in itself since the pairs of opposites that present within the Pleroma—such as fullness and emptiness, living and dead, different and identical, time and space, good and evil, etc.—*cancel each other out in their opposition*. In opposition itself to the Pleroma is the Creature, in its essence, as limited in time and space, and especially differentiated. The feature of differentiation is its very essence; the human being is differentiated and therefore differentiating. This process of differentiation, this struggle against the "dangerous identity of origins",[103] is what the *principium individuationis* consists of, which Jung translated into the process of individuation. Unlike the Pleroma, in which the qualities are present in the form of pairs of opposites that cancel each other out in their opposition, for the Creature, the qualities are differentiated and separated from each other. In the *Seven Sermons*, the Pleroma is taken as a model of the unconscious, even of a proto-unconscious, made up of a set of opposite, but undifferentiated qualities, *awaiting effectuation*, which will be the task of the Creature as a task of differentiation. The task of the Creature, which will later become the task of consciousness, is to bring into existence, *by perceiving them,* the qualities of the Pleroma. In this sense, it creates them. The Creature brings these qualities out of the Pleroma where they were confused. It makes them emerge as pairs of opposites. Moreover, it differentiates itself from these qualities while also producing a discrimination of them.

God himself is Creature. God is posited as a Creature but at the same time as a quality of the Pleroma. God is a manifestation of the Pleroma and an integral part of the manifested world. He is the first specification of the world, but he is not posited as an absolute or as a supreme creative causality. Christine Maillard points out that this concept of the divine is not peculiar to Jung but has Western roots in the negative theology of Master Eckhart and Eastern roots in the Indian religious universe.

The viewpoint of the Sermons is that of the manifestation of the divine in the created world. The Creature is the manifested face of the Pleroma. Here Jung follows a tradition essentially represented in Indian thought for which the world is not conceived as the effect of a contingent creative act but as a necessary reflection of the One in the many.[104]

God is immanent but transcendent in his unmanifest state, the Pleroma. This "relative" God is the Jungian response to the problem of the "death of God" as expressed by Nietzsche. It is the establishment of a new relationship between the human and the divine, subverting the Christian concept but without producing its negation, as is the case in the announcement of the death of God.

Basilides-Philemon's assertion that "God is Creature" must be grasped in its three main implications: the overcoming of a Creator God, the overcoming of theism itself, and the situation within the framework of a negative theology.[105]

God himself is a creature, therefore, and this is enough to remove his power; it is no longer necessary to make him die. But it was precisely to the dead, the not quite dead,[106] that this speech was made by Philemon in *The Red Book*. They, he says, have ended their lives too soon and need to be taught by the living. The issues that Jung feels called to solve come from the dead; the dead hold no additional knowledge, only that held on the day of their death. The dead learn nothing; the dead await the answers that will be given by the living. The dead who harass the living are those who have not accomplished *the principium individuationis*.

The return of the dead comes, in our opinion, in place of a recognition of repetition as a transgenerational problem that wants to repeat what previous generations have not been able to symbolise. It is this return of the same in a new time that the following generations will have to confront, and this is the task that devolves upon them. The process of individuation is therefore the Jungian response to the hazards of transmission. The effect of individuation is to establish new relationships between the subject and the social group.

It implies the passage from a single concept of the divine to a plural concept, as indicated by the task of the Creature, of which God is a stakeholder, namely, to make the qualities of the Pleroma, which are constituted in pairs of opposites, emerge and exist *by perceiving them*. This is how the archetypal world is the product of a fracture and is constituted through the splitting of the One into two (the opposites) after its divide into multiples (the traits or qualities). In this sense, individuation implies the passage from monotheism to polytheism, as the realisation of all the qualities of the Pleroma, in other words, the passage from closure to openness to the "gods" of the unconscious. As C. Maillard again points out:

> The opposition between religious confession and religion, which Jung will not cease to develop and amplify throughout his work, finds its premises in that of monotheism and polytheism exposed in the Sermons. The personal experience of religion can only be polytheistic in nature, since it is, in its very essence, receptivity to the "gods, archetypes-complexes" in the diversity of their deployment from this One, the collective unconscious. Polytheism understood in this way is nothing other than the confrontation with the unconscious, through which the individual becomes what he or she potentially is, in the process of what Jung will call "individuation". Religious experience is then a source of transformation of the individual through contact with the divine world of archetypes.[107]

Monotheism can therefore have as a corollary, massification, due to the hegemony of a single divine principle and the identification of man with the collective consciousness. But polytheism, too, by a sort of return of the repressed contents, can generate psychic epidemics with disastrous consequences. The effect of individuation is to establish new relationships between the subject and the social group. The individual feature of the symbolic experience is the guarantee of its efficiency. When the symbolic life is lived within the framework of a collective myth, this very collectivity is an obstacle to the efficiency of the symbol. It is therefore necessary to avoid both the pitfall of identification with the collective consciousness and that of identification with the collective unconscious. Finally, the idea of the dialectical integration of opposites into a higher-level synthesis would later culminate in the symbolism of *conjunctio*.

> The initiatory path proposed to the dead by Philemon is an erotic one because it is always centred on union, on the bringing together of contrary elements in a middle way that is not a compromise but a transformation of the elements present at the origin.[108]

This middle way, which is elaborated from the opposites, is not that of compromise. It is from a state prior to the formation of the symptom that this path is traced, and of which the symbol is the vector. This path is the one that Jung himself took, faced with the crisis that he went through and circumscribed at the time of the break with Freud (a creative illness if you like), of which *The Red Book* is the witness. Confronted with this de-linking process, he discovered the path of symbols, which he had already sensed as soon as the *Metamorphoses*. This path develops there through the transference supported by the figure of God and into the process of subjectivisation, that is, through the process of individuation. It is from another starting point, that of the symptom, that the Freudian path originates.

Dream and archetype

Symbols from the unconscious layers of the psyche are presented as *variations on a* fundamental *archetypal motif* which can sometimes be traced back through analysis. Cultural, collective symbols relate to eternal truths, and this is the reason for their presence in religious symbolism. Modern man, deprived of this symbolism, sees it re-emerge through dream symbolism. The main task of dreams is to recall this prehistory and the world of childhood, right down to the most primitive instincts. The connection between dream types and mythological themes makes it possible, as Nietzsche did, to make dream thinking a phylogenetic form of our thinking.

For Jung, it is the symbolism of the dream and not the censorship that gives it its encrypted aspect and a different meaning from its apparent content. This "confusion" arises from the fact that the content of the dream is symbolic and, as such, has more than one meaning. The Freud–Jung debate about symbols takes shape here. Symbols are equivocal in themselves and there is no need for Jung to resort to an additional mechanism. In our opinion, censorship can be brought into play in psychic organisations such as neurosis, also giving rise to the formation of symbols even though symbols are not always the effect of censorship. Symbols are a primitive modality of representation or rather *the first modality of representation*. It is their role as a bridge or link, resulting from his work on psychosis that Jung retains. It could be said that symbols in all cases reunite two separated elements, either by repression in Freud's version, where symbols are then a sign of repression, or by dissociation or splitting in Jung's version. In this latter case, symbols achieve the junction, hitherto defective, the reconciliation and the reunion of opposites, hence their role as a link and not as an indication of repression.

The Jungian concept of the archetype results in the highlighting of certain characteristics of the dream.

THE COMPENSATORY AND PROSPECTIVE FUNCTION OF DREAMS

The function of the symbol is itself connected to one of the fundamental characteristics of the unconscious according to Jung, namely, its *compensatory feature*, implied by the drifts of the conscious. The unconscious will manifest itself all the more brutally as the conscious mind moves away from it; it has a "counterbalancing" function. The thoughts, inclinations and tendencies that the conscious life does not sufficiently emphasise or represses or even denies, come into action as if by allusion, during sleep in which the conscious processes are almost totally eliminated.

> In this dream we can discern a compensating function of the unconscious whereby those thoughts, inclinations, and tendencies which in conscious life are too little valued come spontaneously into action during the sleeping state, when the conscious process is to a large extent eliminated.[109]

Dreams then transcribe them, through their own symbolic vocabulary. For Jung, one of the functions of dreams is to allow, *via* their counterbalancing function, restoring the elided part of a representation. This counterbalancing function allows the dreamer to apprehend positively something that seems bad or, conversely, to think negatively of something that seems good. Concluding that something is good or bad depends entirely on our conscious point of view and it is this connection between good and bad that we have to make; nothing is entirely bad nor good and this is how the place of lacking is taken into consideration. Dreams produce the compensation of the conscious situation that gave rise to them. The compensation is not the illusory realisation of a desire, but rather a reality which, if repressed, only asserts itself more:

> If we want to interpret a dream correctly, we need a thorough knowledge of the conscious situation at that moment, because the dream contains its unconscious complement, that is, the material which the conscious situation has constellated in the unconscious [...] As a rule, the unconscious content contrasts strikingly with the conscious material, particularly when the conscious attitude tends too exclusively in a direction that would threaten the vital needs of the individual. The more one-sided his conscious attitude is, and the further it deviates from the optimum, the greater becomes the possibility that vivid dreams with a strongly contrasting but purposive content will appear as an expression of the self-regulation of the psyche.[110]

In the interpretation of dreams, it is therefore a question of confronting dream material with the situation in its actuality. However, Jung does not make his theory of compensation the only law that governs the formation of dreams. The unconscious, like the conscious, is also capable of printing a direction oriented towards an end of which the dream will be the witness. This is in line with Maeder's notion of the prospective activity of dreams. Maeder, who was in correspondence with Freud,[111] set out these conclusions about dreams in a letter to Freud. He supposed that the fulfilment of desire had two aspects: compensation (substitute for what is missing), in accordance with the pleasure principle and a preparatory exercise for the realisable solution of conflicts, in accordance with the reality principle. This second aspect would facilitate the dreamer's adaptation unconsciously. Prospective activity takes the form of an appropriate unconscious function, which, from draft to draft, would prepare the solution of current conflicts and problems through their *representation in symbols,* in anticipation of the conscious activity to come. Dreams produce an anticipation of probabilities, which can, in some cases, be consistent with the real course of events. It could be the scientific basis for the popular belief in the premonitory function of dreams. These two functions, compensatory and prospective, are in reality one and the same. When the compensatory function is exceeded, the prospective function takes over as an outline of a solution to the fracture between conscious and unconscious.

> As against Freud's view that the dream is essentially a wish-fulfilment, I hold with my friend and collaborator Alphonse Maeder that the dream is a spontaneous self-portrayal, in symbolic form, of the actual situation in the unconscious. Our view coincides at this point with the conclusions of Silberer.[112] The agreement with Silberer is the more gratifying in that it came about as the result of mutually independent work.[113]

This independence does not seem certain; Jung's ideas could be based in part on the work of Silberer.[114] Jung considers that his conception of dreams differs from the Freudian one in that it is not concerned with whether or not the contents of the unconscious are wishful thinking. It could be objected that the prospective function includes the perspective of a realisation that a further step could refer to a desire. As is often the case, Jung seeks to demarcate his thinking from that of Freud.

SUBJECT/OBJECT, OR IDENTIFICATION WITH A TRAIT

Jung distinguishes between the interpretation of dreams at the level of the subject and interpretation at the level of the object. The interpretation on the subject level sees in all the figures of the dream the personified traits of the dreamer's personality. The substitution of an unpleasant person for an indifferent one, rather than having the effect of censorship, is for him equivalent to a *depersonalisation* of the affect. As a result, the corresponding libidinal mass has become impersonal; in other words, it is liberated from the personal bond that attached it to its object, which henceforth makes it possible to elevate the previous and real conflict to the level of the subject. Jung gives the example of one of his own dreams. This dream arises in the context of a conflict with Mr. A., whom Jung believes should take all the blame in a case:

> I consulted a lawyer on a certain matter, and to my boundless astonishment he demanded a fee of no less than five thousand francs for the consultation—which I strenuously resisted.[115]

Jung's associations: the lawyer is a colourless reminder of Jung's life as a student, one marked by many arguments. The lawyer's abruptness is reminiscent of A.'s and their ongoing conflict. One could deduce that behind the lawyer is A. In his youth, a student with no resources had asked Jung to lend him 5000 francs. A. would be assimilated into the image of this needy student, a beginner, whose opinions would be questionable. This would, therefore, reassure Jung that his position towards A. was well-founded. But Jung wakes up in anger about the lawyer's claims. He associates the lawyer with procedural disputes and his own stubbornness to be right all the time. If the dispute with A. drags on, it is because his own reasoning self refuses to give up. All this played a role in the conflict with A. The interpretation at the level of the subject is much more fruitful. The interpretation at the level of the object, attributing the traits in question to the object itself, is opposed to the interpretation at the level of the subject, in principle. In reality, these two aspects, as Jung acknowledges, are intertwined and it is rather a question of knowing which one prevails.

This is, once again, another way of formulating *the identification with a trait*. It is the modality of identification that is prevalent in dreams and just as frequent in the conflict. This interpretation of dreams is classically Freudian except that Jung adds his own touch or, rather, his personal reformulation, which differentiates between interpretation at the level of the subject and interpretation at the level of the object. It should be noted in passing that it is important for Jung to differentiate these two terms, the subject from the object, through the identification that links them. Nevertheless, Jung emphasises an important point when he speaks of the depersonalisation of affect. The depersonalisation of affect links together the two levels of interpretation. The work of the dream aims at this depersonalisation which allows the dreamer to *make a judgement on the trait itself (in this case, to be always right) and the necessary adjustment, i.e. a work on the drive that underlies it*. Jung applies these same considerations to the analysis of transference. The analyst needs to know what is his own real part in the dynamics of the transference and what is the projected part of the analysand. It is a question of navigating between two pitfalls, that of systematically reducing the transference to infantile wishes and that of taking the transference at face value.

THE DREAM SERIES

Jung insists that the symbolism of dreams must not be considered in a semiotic way; symbols must not be attributed a fixed meaning. The symbols of dreams are expressions of contents that the conscious mind has not yet grasped; moreover, they must be considered from the point of view of their relativity, depending on the momentary conscious situation. In theory, there are symbols whose meaning is more or less fixed, without which it would be impossible to specify anything about the structure of the unconscious, but in practice, however, they are always to be handled *relatively*. Without this indeterminacy, these symbols would not be symbols but signs or symptoms. The sign is a perceived phenomenon that manifests a non-perceived phenomenon, like smoke for fire. Its own content is always more limited than the concept it represents, unlike the symbol. The idea of the Trinity, for example, is a symbol, not a sign. It is a form, a figure and an image that approaches an unknown thing apprehended by intuition.

Jung gave the example of the beginning of the treatment of a patient, the son of a peasant, who became a professor and reached the top of the social ladder. The patient reported a set of symptoms resembling altitude sickness. He mentioned two dreams he had the night before the consultation:

A first dream takes the dreamer back to his home village. He pretends not to recognise a group of peasants with whom he went to school and passes them. He hears one of them saying: "It is not often that he comes back to the village". This dream reminds him of the humility of his beginnings but also of his forgetfulness. In a second dream, he is in a great hurry because he is going on a trip; the train will soon leave. He realises that he has forgotten his briefcase containing important papers and hurriedly goes back to get it. Indeed, when he arrives, the train leaves the station. The rails make a peculiar S-shaped curve. It is a very long curve and the patient thinks that if the engineer gives full steam while the trailing cars are still on the curve, the train may derail. It "snakes", prefiguring the dragon figure that will appear later … Indeed, the engineer gives full steam and the train derails. The patient wakes up, distressed.

The patient, Jung tells us, describes through the dream the haste with which he always tries to go forward but, as in the case of the train driver who advances without worrying about what follows, a loss of balance occurs, equivalent to his neurosis. Mountain sickness is the symbolic representation of an ascent exhaustion and the dream confirms this hypothesis as the aetiology of the neurosis. In a third dream, the dreamer is on the farm of an unknown peasant woman. He tells her about a long journey to Leipzig that he plans to make on foot and she looks at him admiringly. He himself is looking out of the window at this moment, contemplating the landscape;

reapers are at work. Suddenly, in the background, a huge crayfish or lizard appears and moves to the left and then to the right, so that the dreamer finds himself caught in the angle of these two movements. He then realises that he is holding a magic wand in his hand; he strikes the monster with it and it dies immediately. Standing next to the corpse, the dreamer looks at it for a long time. He then wakes up.

The patient made the following associations: the farmhouse evokes the hospice of Saint-Jacques, where, in 1444, 1500 confederates died heroically for not respecting orders to wait for reinforcements. Here we find the idea of the rush forward and its fatal consequences, already expressed in the second dream. The peasant woman reminds him of a landlady, an uneducated woman with whom he chats from time to time. The long journey to Leipzig reminds him of the great enterprise he has in mind as he has to get there on foot, by himself. The woman's astonishment refers to his overly modest environment (Jung adds that this is probably an inferiority felt by the subject himself). The image of the reapers evokes a painting he owns.

The angle formed by the movements in which he is standing represents his mother's legs between which he is placed, having just been born or aspiring to return to her womb.

The crayfish has the peculiarity of swimming backwards (in fact sideways). In the dream, it seems to be looking to find its way. The fight with the monster evokes the struggle of the hero and the dragon.

Jung makes the following interpretation: the dreamer is brought back to his modest origins, then to the danger of haste and a simple way to avoid it. He reacts by turning to a hero figure in order to compensate for a feeling of inferiority, first by the allusion to the battle of the hospice of Saint James, but in a second stage, a displacement occurs on the mythical level. The dreamer compensates for the feeling of inferiority linked to his origins by identifying with the character of the hero. A human destiny is then enlarged to the proportions of a mythological problem, as for example in Egyptian medicine.[116] This mythology of the collective unconscious is characterised, according to Jung, by a kind of flow that naturally causes a new theme to emerge from a finite motif. As a result, there is no longer any stagnation.[117] The danger, personified by the monster or the dragon, a mythical figure if ever there was one, is at first taken lightly and even rendered *insignificant*; a wave of the magic wand is enough to neutralise it. The half-crayfish, half-lizard monster is one of the original archetypal images. The figure of the saurian is already present in the second dream, which makes the train "snake" before leading it to disaster. The dreamer's body in fact escapes his control and reacts with symptoms, of which the monster could constitute the metaphorical representation. He would have had to meet the dragon, Jung tells us, because the dragon, like the hero, is a centre charged with energy. But, when the monster appears, the misrecognition continues as the dreamer neutralises it with a wave of his magic wand rendering it *insignificant*. The personal unconscious of the dreamer requires associations. For the collective unconscious, it is different. The symbols used are those that generally leave patients short of associations:

> What he had mentioned before were all things which you could meet with in real life, things which do actually exist. But the crab is not a personal experience, it is an archetype. When an analyst has to deal with an archetype he may begin to think. In dealing with the personal unconscious you are not allowed to think too much and to add anything to the associations of the patient [...] The other individual has a life of his own and a mind of his own inasmuch as he is a person. But in as much as he is not a person, inasmuch as he is also myself, he has the same basic structure of mind, and there I can begin to think, I can associate for him. I can even provide him with the necessary context because he will have none, he does not know where that crab-lizard comes from and has no idea what it means, but I know and can provide the material for him.[118]

Here, we touch on what makes the Jungian approach specific and, undoubtedly, its limits. Jung considers that, faced with an archetypal motif (an element of the collective unconscious), the analyst's associations are as useful as those of the dreamer. This aspect will become prevalent in his technique of dream interpretation to the point of neglecting the so-called personal unconscious of the dreamer. Another essential aspect of his method consists in the interest in the *succession of symbols* because, as we said, symbols must not be interpreted in isolation but in their association with other symbols. This led Jung to ask his patients to keep a dream diary and to come to the session with their written dreams and their context. Indeed, the interpretation only achieves relative assurance during *a series of dreams* because the fundamental themes and motifs acquire a much more marked relief.

Jung sees the symptom as a shoot above the ground, emerging from the main plant, which is itself structured as a rhizome,[119] a very extensive underground root system and which constitutes the content of the neurosis and the very matrix of complexes, symptoms and dreams. This is why, generally, *a dream belongs to a series of dreams. There is a continuity of unconscious processes* and dreams are the visible links in a chain of unconscious events. What makes Jung's interpretation of dreams so special, and what is similar to our own approach, is that it proceeds from a succession of dreams, from a series:

> As a rule a dream belongs in a series. Since there is a continuity of consciousness despite the fact that it is regularly interrupted by sleep, there is probably also a continuity of unconscious processes perhaps even more than with the events of consciousness. In any case my experience is in favour of the probability that dreams are the visible links in a chain of unconscious events.[120]

The dreams belonging to a series are in fact linked together in a very significant way. The series is not chronologically ordered but connected to a centre from which the dreams radiate. A new theme may appear and then disappear in favour of an earlier theme.

> The true configuration of dreams is radial: dreams radiate from a centre, and only then do they submit to our perception of time. Dreams are in fact subordinate to *a central core of meaning.*[121]

Among the analyses recounted by Jung, that of the physicist Wolfgang Pauli, whose name was later revealed, has a special place. The personality of the analysand, a physicist renowned for his work in quantum mechanics for which he was awarded the Nobel Prize in Physics, is not unrelated to this. But this analysis is also characterised by the abundance of his dreams. Jung studied them in their sequential aspect in *Psychology and Alchemy*[122] and also returned to some of them in the *Terry Lectures.*[123]

The patient was first entrusted to a junior analyst; Jung only received him in the final part of the treatment. The material consists of over a thousand dreams of which Jung used the first 400. In *Psychology and Alchemy*, Jung first extracted the initial 22 dreams. He sought to show the extent to which the symbolism of the mandala, taken from Tibetan Buddhism, appeared early and was embedded in the dream material. In a second step, he extracted, in chronological order, the dreams that were particularly related to what he defined as the mandala figure. For Jung, it was after an initial phase in which "the patient's spiritual presuppositions" became clear that a second phase occurred. This second phase was marked by the production of symbols of unity,[124] which Jung calls mandalas and which appear in dreams or in the form of visual impressions. These symbols had a compensatory function with regard to the contradictions and conflicts of the conscious situation. This phase of the process was marked by the production of symbols of unity, the so-called mandalas:

> This phase of the process is marked by the production of symbols of unity, the so called mandalas, which occur either in dreams or in the form of concrete visual impressions, often as the most obvious compensation of the contradictions and conflicts of the conscious situation.[125]

It is the successive production of these symbols that Jung refers to as the "individuation process". The path followed by this process is not a straight line but rather a kind of spiral. The dream themes constantly lead back to a centre and come closer and closer to it:

> The way is not straight but appears to go round in circles. More accurate knowledge has proved it to go in spirals: the dream-motifs always return

after certain intervals to definite forms, whose characteristic it is to define a centre. And as a matter of fact the whole process revolves about a central point or some arrangement round a centre, which may in certain circumstances appear even in the initial dreams. As manifestations of unconscious processes the dreams rotate or circumambulate round the centre, drawing closer to it as the amplifications increase in distinctness and in scope.[126]

The dream symbols of the individuation process are thus the support of an ordering and centring, and of constituting a new centre of the personality. Jung calls this centre the Self, conceived as the totality of the psyche, which includes both the conscious and unconscious. The Self is the centre of this totality as the ego is the centre of consciousness. Symbols that relate directly to the awareness of this centre fall into this particular category that Jung calls mandala symbolism.[127] Note that these images appear at the point where thought is lacking. They are always quaternary systems. *The unconscious process thus spirals around a centre and slowly moves towards it.* The symbols present at the beginning of the process reappear in successive waves, thus repeating themselves. Here, for us, Jung calls symbols those same linguistic elements that Lacanian analysts would call signifiers, or rather pre-signifiers if we consider the production of significance as a progressive process, and as appearing in a recurrent manner in the series of dreams. Their denotation as symbols refer, for Jung, to their function of reconciling opposites. Their progressive integration by consciousness results in their reappearance in an amplified manner. This is the progress of the cure. The centre acts like a magnet on the materials of the unconscious and gradually captures them as in a crystalline network, like spiders web. In fact, new connections appear between these symbol-signifiers and the network structure that organises them gradually takes shape.[128]

Dreams are presented in *Psychology and Alchemy* in an abbreviated form, excluding all personal elements, for the sake of discretion. This work of synthesis of the unconscious would have been even more perceptible, Jung tells us, if the material concerning the intimate life of the subject had not had to be subtracted for the same reasons already mentioned. Jung does not indicate any contextual elements and proceeds exactly as if he himself were the author of the dreams. This approach, which he admits to being aberrant in the case of isolated dreams, is justified by the fact that these are series of dreams, internally linked, through the course of which the meaning gradually develops on its own. The series is precisely the context provided by the dreamer himself. It is as if there is not one text but *many texts that shed light on each other.* In fact, Pauli's dreams show an obvious recurrence of motifs whose arrangement varies from one dream to another. Nevertheless, Jung's decision to remove elements of an individual nature deprives us of any possibility of analysis. Jung refers to the need for discretion, which is all the more imperative as Pauli is in some way a public figure. This necessity does not hide the fact that, for Jung, the main subject of interest lies in the "collective" motifs. The repetition of these motifs is all the more clearly highlighted by this bias. Jung, as usual, produces an archetypal interpretation of them, which leads him to articulate the motifs produced in comparison with those of the symbolism within different traditions. But he also sees, in the progression of the treatment, the development of the mandala figure. This corresponds to an archetype that manifests itself from the beginning and subsequently with greater clarity and frequency as the dreams progress. It should be remembered that for Jung, the appearance of successive symbols is based, at each stage, on the conscious handling of an unconscious element. It is this articulation between the conscious and the unconscious that constitutes the progress of the treatment and this is why he considers it to be a work of synthesis.

The serial analysis of dreams constitutes for us one of the most interesting elements of Jungian thinking; it is consistent with our clinical experience. The systematic transcription of dreams in the course of an analysis, as we shall return to, makes it possible to highlight the recurrence of certain motifs, inserted each time in a different context, and clarifying, because of their insertion in different semantic fields, the connections between these fields. This method leads to a deciphering analogous to that of Egyptian hieroglyphics, a deciphering that no other method would have made it possible, a direct deciphering by free association being excluded.

Freud's "Father"

It is from the dreams, the royal road, but also from another starting point, the symptom of neurosis, that Freud deals with the question of symbols. But he also approaches the question of collective symbolism, in his own way, combining the symbolism of dreams and the murder of the Father.

The symbolism of dreams

The distortion of dreams, according to Freud, is not only the result of the action of censorship but also of a second factor, the symbolism of dreams. This idea appears for the first time in *The Interpretation of Dreams*[129] and is developed in the *Introductory Lectures on Psychoanalysis*.[130] The essence of the symbolic relationship is a comparison whose *tertium comparationis* is not always obvious. There is a common trait between the symbol and the term it symbolises. But the role of comparison is limited in several ways. In dreams, only some of the latent thoughts are concerned with the comparison which itself is not necessarily recognised by the subject; moreover, a comparison is not enough to generate a symbol. The comparison is a constitutive element of the symbol but cannot by itself account for it. Several symbols can have an identical content and conversely a symbol can refer to several different elements so that a relation with the question of condensation is therefore appearing. Dream symbolism is characterised by both synonymy and polysemy. Symbols are determined only insofar as they maintain multiple relationships with the text that carries them.

These relationships are underpinned by two kinds of symbolism: individual symbolism and universal symbolism. Hence, the combination in *The Interpretation of Dreams* of two techniques, two methods of dream interpretation: *The method of deciphering* (specific to psychoanalysis): it treats the dream as a cipher where each sign is translated, thanks to free association. The images of the dream need to be translated into words in order to find what Freud calls the thoughts[131] of the dream, those that allowed the dream to be constructed, thanks to the processes of figuration, displacement and condensation.

The symbolic method: it proceeds from the knowledge of symbols, constant symbols, such as can be found in the various productions of culture. This technique is held by Freud to be auxiliary. From the beginning of his work, Freud noted the presence inside certain dreams of "fixed" symbols, for which associations are lacking. Between 1900 (first edition) and 1914, an independent section on symbolism was gradually added to the *Interpretation of Dreams*. Freud repeatedly called for research into symbols. Initially, he considered drawing up a kind of dictionary of symbols, then, in 1910, he asked Jung[132] to resume this research, but this time through a history of language and myth.

However, we can think, alongside Laplanche,[133] that the symbolism of dreams is introduced in the first edition of the Traumdeutung with the notion of *typical dreams*, even before all the subsequent development on the symbolism of dreams that will be integrated into the following editions. Laplanche proposes an interesting comparison between this type of symbolism and the secondary elaboration:

> In dreams, we can imagine at least three levels. What Freud sometimes calls the "dream undertaking", which we would call nowadays the "promotion", the setting up: this is the level of the drive, which is the promoter of the dream; a level of implementation: what is described to us as the work of the dream; finally a level of "facade", of finishing, where all this work is put into shape one last time to be represented. Now, as much with regard to symbolism as to certain types of secondary elaboration, one could sometimes have the impression of a sort of short-circuiting of the intermediate phase (that of the work), of a sort of direct crossing of an unconscious content (here, par excellence, the Oedipus complex) through the layers that are usually those of psychic elaboration.

These typical dreams, present in all of us, would have common origins and would have the same feature, indicative of this universal symbolism, of not leading to any association and therefore of falling under symbolic interpretation rather than associative interpretation. Among these typical dreams are *dreams of the death of loved ones.* In the case of these dreams, Freud tells us, the disguise is absent, only the affect is modified. There are actually two types of such dreams: those in which the affect is neutral, indifferent, and those accompanied by a painful affect. Dreams where the affect is one of indifference are not typical and refer to a desire other than that of the death of a loved one. On the contrary, dreams with painful affect are directly related to the death of these people. These dreams have the meaning of their content, but with the reversal of affect, they betray the wish to see these people die. What is notable is that *these dreams are associated with Freud's elaboration of the Oedipus complex*, which is directly related to the symbolic function:

> There is an unmistakable indication in the text of Sophocles' tragedy itself that the legend of Oedipus sprang from some primaeval dream-material which had as its content the distressing disturbance of a child's relation to his parents owing to the first stirrings of sexuality. At a point when Oedipus, though he is not yet enlightened, has begun to feel troubled by his recollection of the oracle, Jocasta consoles him by referring to a dream which many people dream, though, as she thinks, it has no meaning:

> "Many a man ere now in dreams hath lain
> With her who bare him. He hath least annoy
> Who with such omens troubleth not his mind"

> Today, just as then, many men dream of having sexual relations with their mothers, and speak of the fact with indignation and astonishment. It is clearly the key to the tragedy and the complement to the dream of the dreamer's father being dead.[134]

The "fixed' symbolism is expressed clinically by the analysand's silence or the absence of associations concerning a few elements of the dream. Freud produced an almost exhaustive catalogue of these "ready-made" symbols in the *Traumdeutung* (the house for the body, etc.).[135] We are then tempted, he says, to translate them by our own means. This is also, as we have seen, Jung's position with regard to "collective" symbols. We then obtain constant translations, quite similar to those in popular dream books. It is this constant relationship between an element of the dream and its translation that is considered by Freud as typical of the collective symbolism. For Freud, the majority of dream collective symbols are so-called "sexual" symbols.[136] A lot of objects are reviewed. In fact, nothing or almost nothing escapes this sexual symbolism to the point that the term sexual, designating here the difference between male and female organs or the allusion to sexual relations, loses its impact. Freud agrees with this lending himself to the criticism that Jung will level at him. So to what do we owe this knowledge of symbolism, since it is not provided to us by the associations of the dreamer? We owe it to myths, tales, folklore, etc. Here Freud joins Jung. In fact, the whole sum of knowledge resulting from the collective experience makes the treasure and the spring of language. As Michel Arrivé points out: "The objects listed by Freud are semiotic objects: either discourses (tales and myths, jokes and pranks, proverbs and songs), or practices (mores and customs), or languages: poetic language and common language".[137]

The dreamer thus has at his disposal a mode of symbolic expression that he neither knows nor recognises in the waking state:

> In the first place we are faced with the fact that the dreamer has a symbolic mode of expression at his disposal which he does not know in waking life and does not recognize. This is as extraordinary as if you were to discover that your housemaid understood Sanskrit, though you know that she was born in a Bohemian village and never learnt it [...] Now, however, it is a question of more than this, of unconscious pieces of knowledge, of connections of thought, of comparisons between different objects which result in its being possible for one of them to be *regularly*[138] put in place of the other.[139]

This symbolism would consist of an ancient mode of expression, which has practically disappeared except for the remains that testify to its survival, and Freud gives as an example the "basic" Schreberian language in which this symbolism manifests itself without being identified as such:

> One gets an impression that what we are faced with here is an ancient but extinct mode of expression, of which different pieces have survived in different fields, one piece only here, another only there, a third, perhaps, in slightly modified forms in several fields. And here I recall the phantasy of an interesting psychotic patient, who imagined a "basic language" of which all these symbolic relations would be residues.[140]

Symbolism would have to do with the survival of linguistic identities during the development of language. It would be a vestige of the old word identity.

> Things that are symbolically connected to-day were probably united in prehistoric times by conceptual and linguistic identity. The symbolic relation seems to be a relic and a mark of former identity.[141]

At the same time, Freud published the article *The Antithetical Meanings of Primal Words,*[142] indicating the presence in ancient Egyptian of words with two opposite meanings, as also found in dreams. The later evolution of the language would have made it possible to discriminate between each of the meanings by adding a sign to indicate which meaning is preferred. He introduces this article with a quote from *The Interpretation of Dreams*:

> The way in which dreams treat the category of contraries and contradicto-ries is highly remarkable. It is simply disregarded. 'No' seems not to exist so far as dreams are concerned. They show a particular preference for combining contraries into a unity or for representing them as one and the same thing. Dreams feel themselves at liberty, moreover, to represent any element by its wishful contrary; so that there is no way of deciding at a first glance whether any element that admits of a contrary is present in the dream-thoughts as a positive or as a negative.[143]

The mechanisms of dream work would correspond to those at play in the evolution of language. Symbolism is thus conceived, in Freud, as in Jung, as a residue, but in Freud, it is a *residue of the work operating in language*. It is therefore from this work of the language, woven into the social group, that the deformation of dreams inherent in symbolism borrows its contours. Freudian collective symbolism is therefore not Jungian collective symbolism. On the one hand (for Jung), there is an inherited representative potentiality, in a state of provisional, reversible lack of differentiation, only asking to be embodied in a symbol, but awaiting its assumption by the individual differentiated con-sciousness, see *The Red Book*. On the other hand (for Freud), there is a residue presented as that of the unfinished work of language in the group, fixing one of the pieces of the symbol, which the subject cannot associate with, in a collective unconscious, but whose collective essence is to be found in the materials of myths, tales, etc. In both cases, there is a link with the collective unconscious but it is presented in a different way: on the one hand, there is a "first" collective unconscious in the state of traces, awaiting singularisation, in order to be integrated into a personal history. On the other hand, there is a personal history with the persistence of encysted residues of the collective unconscious, rendered in terms of the history of language.

Alongside the symbolism of dreams, Freud uses the term symbolic in another way. The term "symbolic" is used to designate, in a general way, the relationship between the manifest content of a behaviour, a thought or a word and its latent meaning. Following Freud, several authors (Rank, Sachs, Ferenczi and Jones) affirmed that in psychoanalysis one can only speak of symbolism when the symbolised is unconscious. This other meaning of symbolism in Freud is connected to the question of the symptom.

The symbolism of the symptom

The symbolism of the symptom was first introduced with the notion of a *mnemic symbol*. The notion of the mnemic symbol appeared around 1895. It then disappeared and reappeared 30 years later in *Inhibition, Symptom and*

Anxiety, published in 1926. The term "mnemic symbol" was produced in the beginning of Freud's work alongside the notions of trauma and "irreconcilability" in relation to neurosis and, first of all, to conversion hysteria:

> The conversion may be either total or partial. It proceeds along the line of the motor or sensory innervation which is related—whether intimately or more loosely—to the traumatic experience. By this means the ego succeeds in freeing itself from the contradiction [with which it is confronted]; but instead, it has burdened itself with a *mnemic symbol*[144] which finds a lodgement in consciousness, like a sort of parasite, either in the form of an unresolvable motor innervation or as a constantly recurring hallucinatory sensation, and which persists until a conversion in the opposite direction takes place.[145]

In *The Aetiology of Hysteria*, Freud poses the problem of the relationship between symptom and symbol:

> If we try, in an approximately similar way, to induce the symptoms of a hysteria to make themselves heard as witnesses to the history of the origin of the illness, we must take our start from Josef Breuer's momentous discovery: *the symptoms of hysteria* (apart from the stigmata) *are determined by certain experiences of the patient's which have operated in a traumatic fashion and which are being reproduced in his psychical life in the form of mnemic symbols.*[146]

The mnemic symbol constitutes an element of determination of the symptom in its specificity. Nevertheless, for there to be a symbol, there must be a trace, a memory trace, of a traumatic event.[147] The symbol and the memory trace are linked. The mechanism of symbolisation implies that the literal meaning of a figurative expression is put into action. For example, the expression "getting slapped", in the figurative sense, is expressed as facial neuralgia.[148] By taking a figurative expression literally, the hysterical person does not take the words lightly, she relives once again the sensations that justify the verbal expression in question as a product of the work of language in the social group. The symptom of hysteria and the usual language are reciprocally linked through a third term, a common source which is a primitive, basic language.

In connection with the term "mnemic symbol" comes the notion of symbolisation, to be understood here as *the formation of a symptom under the effect of a symbolic process*. Symbolisation appears in the *Studies on Hysteria* as one of the two processes that allow the formation of symptoms. The other mechanism involves contiguity or simultaneity. In phobia and obsessional neurosis, there is no conversion but a transposition. It is through transposition that the affect connected to the irreconcilable representation is detached from the representation. This is a process. It is *the process of symbolisation*. But, as much as the term symbol is redundant in Freud when attached to dream symbolism, the adjective symbolic is rare. This is because Freud is describing a process, the process of symbolisation, but the term symbolic is replaced by terms such as symptom formation or substitute formation. The question then arises as to whether the process of symbolisation and the process of symptom formation can legitimately be equated as "symbolic" formations.

Let us take the case of the phobia of the horse in little Hans. The repression concerns not one but several instinctual impulses: a hostile impulse is directed against the father, coexisting with a passive tender motion, that is, Freud[149] says, the desire to be loved by the father as an object in the sense of genital eroticism. All this is also accompanied by a tender motion towards the mother. The repression concerns the impulse motion and its representatives. Alongside the repression of the representation, it is necessary to consider something else that represents the drive and undergoes a different destiny. The term "quantum of affect" designates this other element of the psychic representative; it corresponds to the drive, insofar as it has detached itself from the representation and finds an expression in accordance with its quantity in processes that are felt in the form of affects.[150] The term "mnemic symbol" is reintroduced at the beginning of *Inhibition, Symptom and Anxiety* in connection with the affect:

> Affective states have become incorporated in the mind as precipitates of primaeval traumatic experiences, and when a similar situation occurs they are revived like *mnemic symbols.*[151,152]

According to M. Arrivé,[153] one could say that the quantum of affect represents (symbolises) the drive. But also that the representative represents (symbolises) the drive and again that anguish represents (symbolises) the affect linked to the repressed drive. We could also say that the horse represents (symbolises) the father and that the feared bad treatment from him represents (symbolises) castration. The different meanings of the symbol would be brought together. Symbolism is thus both referred to the drive and to the one who is the holder. Freud is primarily concerned with *who* the symbol is a substitute for, rather than simply the bearer of a drive's trait. For him, totemism provides the junction between the two:

> Wild beasts are as a rule employed by the dream-work to represent passionate impulses of which the dreamer is afraid, whether they are his own or those of other people. (It then needs only a slight displacement for the wild beasts to come to represent the people who are possessed by these passions. We have not far to go from here to cases in which a dreaded father is represented by a beast of prey or a dog or wild horse—a form of

representation recalling totemism.) It might be said that the wild beasts are used to represent the libido, a force dreaded by the ego and combated by means of repression.[154]

We are thus faced with an apparently heterogeneous conception of the symbol. On the one hand, the dream symbol is either an individual elementa figuration of a latent, repressed element that free association is, nonetheless, able to recover, or else it is a collective one, also a figuration of a latent element, but an archaic one and a consequence of the evolution of language, which the history of the evolution of language would allow us to clarify. On the other hand, it is the symbol–symptom, a figuration not of an equivalent element, but *of a mnemic trace, a drive trace of traumatic origin*, which finds in the symptom a modality of direct representation, a short circuit, which makes deciphering more difficult. What is the relationship between the formation of symbols of the "horse" type, as in Hans, and the formation of symbols at work in language? For Freud, the symbol is above all the individual symbol—that of the dream or that of the symptom. The articulation of the symbol to the social group is not formulated as such; Freud's way of entry into the collective universe is the murder of the father.

Murder of the father and the social group

The path from the social group to the individual passes, for Freud, through the murder of the father of the horde and his incorporation, as described in *Totem and Taboo*. This path continues through the primary identification with the "father" in *Collective Psychology and Analysis of the Ego*, with the appearance of the Ego-ideal and its re-elaboration in *The Ego and the Id*. The murder of the Father, as seen in the history of religion version, will finally be taken up again in *Moses and Monotheism*.

TOTEM AND TABOO[155]

The taboo is directly related to the ambivalence of feelings. The word taboo itself brings together opposing notions: that of the sacred and that of the dangerous, the forbidden or the impure. The word taboo itself is an ambivalent word. What is forbidden can only be what is desired; the taboo is to be considered the root of the law. Among the taboo's different objects is the taboo of the dead. The taboo of the dead is linked to the fear of their possible return. In fact, the death of a loved one has satisfied an unconscious desire which, if it had been powerful enough, would have caused the death itself. The taboo is a sign of the inadequacy of the separation from the dead and the failure to mourn. The taboo can also affect the name of the dead, which is forbidden to be uttered, and which, in the case where this name is also that of an animal or an object, can generate an instability of vocabulary.

The taboo is a sign of the ambivalence of human affectivity; it constitutes a symptom of compromise between the two tendencies. It manifests itself in the prohibition to kill the totem animal and to have sexual relations with individuals of the same totem. It is a manifestation of the law of the totem and thus organises social relations. The totem is transmitted through the maternal line and is the basis for exogamy. It is endowed with qualities that are often those of animals and it bears witness to the descent of these animals. It is a kind of ancestor; in fact, the totemic animal is a product of the transformation of the human soul. The totem embodies the community; it identifies the community as such. It differs from the fetish in that it is never a single object but the representative of a species. It is representative of *a group with which man identifies*.

For Freud, as for Jung, animism is not a vanished belief belonging to a primitive era that has passed. Primitive animism is found in the attitude of the child. His attitude towards animals does not draw a line between human and animal kingdoms. The identification with the animal and the ambivalent attitude towards it are the roots of infantile animal phobias which are based on the persistence of these totemic residues. Obsessive neurosis takes up the structure of the taboo, being itself at the foundation of the religion that followed animism in social evolution. The totemic residues of phobia, the taboos of obsessional neurosis, and the figuration of conversion hysteria all allow us to see in the symptom a kind of archaic isolate, a vestige of the animist period. The opposition of tendencies characterising the taboo is identical to that found in obsessive patients. But in this case, one of the terms of the opposition is repressed and remains unconscious while the other manifests itself with obsessive force. Even more generally, the two prescriptions of totemism—the prohibition to kill the totem animal as well as the prohibition to have sexual relations with a partner of the same totem—coincide with the Oedipal crimes.[156]

The Freudian conjecture of the primitive horde's murder of the father is based on the work of Robertson Smith and the substitution of the father for the totemic animal. The totemic meal, for its part, constitutes what allows the assimilation, or the appropriation, of the father's qualities. In fact, it is above all an appropriation of qualities of which the totem, like the father, is only the vector, *these qualities also being those of a group*, testifying to the individual's belonging to this group. Without the hypothesis of a collective soul, of a continuity of man's psychic life, despite the death of individuals, collective psychology could not exist.

Even the most ruthless suppression must leave room for distorted surrogate impulses and for reactions resulting from them. If so, however, we may safely assume that no generation is able to conceal any of its more important mental processes from its successor. For psycho-analysis has shown us that everyone possesses in his unconscious mental activity an apparatus which enables him to interpret other people's reactions, that is to undo the distortions which other people have imposed on the expression of their feelings. An unconscious understanding such as this of all the customs, ceremonies and dogmas left behind by the original relation to the father may have made it possible for later generations to take over their heritage of emotion.[157]

IDENTIFICATION WITH A TRAIT: THE HINGE BETWEEN THE INDIVIDUAL AND
THE COLLECTIVE

In 1921, Freud extended the ideas in *Totem and Taboo* in his article *Group Psychology and Analysis of the Ego*. From the outset, he introduced the idea that, because of its constant interaction with the other, individual psychology is also a social psychology. We thus immediately find the terms that run throughout the debate with Jung. For Freud, the insertion into a crowd modifies the psyche of the individual, except in organised crowds where his own characteristics remain. Love relationships constitute the essence of the soul of crowds. In artificial crowds such as the church and the army, each isolated individual is libidinally linked to the leader on the one hand, and to the other individuals in the crowd on the other hand. An idea, a tendency *or a common trait can take the place of the leader.* This issue is found in the family where identification with the leader is realised in the form of identification with the father.

Freud developed also his concept of identification. The primordial identification with the father is an exemplary identification built on the model of the Ideal. It is the offspring of the first oral cannibalistic phase, where one incorporates the coveted object and in so doing, annihilates it. This identification is an identification with what one would like to be, as opposed to the choice of the object, which one would like to have. In identification, the object has been lost or renounced; it is then restored inside the ego. In love, the object is preserved and over-invested. It is idealised by the ego and at its own expense. However, certain scenarios carry out the conjunction of love and identification. A primary crowd is the sum of individuals who put one and the same object in the place of their Ego-ideal and are, consequently, identified with each other. In the family, the eldest child is forced to identify with the other children and thus the feeling of a crowd is formed which replaces jealousy: "The social feeling is thus based on the reversal of a feeling that was initially hostile into a positive link, of the nature of an identification".[158] The crowd thus appears as a revival of the original horde, just like in the family. Here, Freud takes up the elements of *Totem and Taboo*. Crowd psychology is the oldest psychology of man from which individual psychology partially emerged later. As we have seen, this is also what Jung said about it. The father of the horde, absolutely narcissistic, forced his sons, so to speak, to enter into the psychology of the crowd up to the point of murder, for which the totemic ban was responsible for maintaining the memory and symbolising the expiation. The crowd is equivalent to the horde of brothers. In the crowd, the individual abandons his Ego-ideal and exchanges it for the ideal of the crowd, embodied by the leader. The leader of the crowd embodies the original father, himself a divine prefiguration; he is this ideal of the crowd that dominates the Ego in place of the Ego-ideal.

On this basic configuration, the artificial crowd constituted by the church goes a step further, Freud tells us: it demands more. It establishes a minimum of organisation. The Christian loves Christ as his ideal and feels bound to other Christians by identification. So far, nothing more. But the Christian must also identify with Christ and love other Christians as Christ had loved them. Identification must be added where the object choice occurred (Christ) and love where the identification was (other Christians). It is through identification with Christ, but rather, in fact, through identification with that trait initially carried by him, "the love of Christians", that the primitive rivalry is neutralised. But other outcomes are possible and Freud invokes Rank's *The Myth of the Hero* to outline the path of the hero, incarnation of the Ego-ideal, who wants to be alone to accomplish the task devolved to the horde of brothers. The myth, a creation of the poet, could be the step that allows the individual to leave crowd psychology and to offer his audience another support for identification. However, this outcome could well be partly the same as the previous one; isn't the hero the precursor of the later return of the father in the form of a deity? The hero, this figure of the Ideal, carries out the murder alone. He claims, in his pride, to do without the group; he is only a masked figure of the father. Freud, taking up the figure of the hero, joins the Jung of the *Metamorphoses*.[159]

In Freud, the primary identification that will give rise to the Ego-ideal is again taken up, in 1923, in *The Ego and the Id*.[160] The primordial identification with the "father" is, rather, a more global identification with the other. It is an identification with the parents before sexual difference occurs; Freud says it predates any object investment. Subsequently, the reorganisations linked to the Oedipal situation will make the Ego-ideal, which is not distinguished from the Superego yet, a two-faced instance, the site of conflict and the matrix of repression. Let us note that this aspect is in a way secondary if we consider its birth as anterior, a stigma of the oral incorporation of the "father", with its oedipal superstructure being added subsequently. There are, therefore, two moments for the construction of this instance:

A pre-oedipal time, under the auspices of the oral incorporation of the "father", assimilated there to the parents, in fact to the other. This is the incarnation of the collective, the first mark of the seal of language and of the emergence of the subject.

Then there is an Oedipal period with its reorganisations translated by the dialectic of love and identification which will make up the Ego-ideal this trait[161] likely to provoke love that the subject will cultivate within himself or that he will seek in the other of the love bond or that of the leader of the crowd.

This is the point where the individual and the collective come together. This double process of idealisation and identification, i.e. the conjunction of the formation of an ideal within the ego and the tendency to reproduce the ideal in different subjects belonging to a given group, constitutes the theoretical grid that allows us to think, without rupture, of the belonging of the individual and the group.[162] For Jung, this point of juncture, of meeting between the individual and the collective, is just as actively sought after but it will be found in the symbol. The Jungian symbol is at this junction. It is a way out of narcissism, but *a way of doing without the cult of the father or the organisation of crowds*. However, it comes at the expense of the identification of the unary trait and its consequences.

MURDER OF MOSES

Freud returned to the collective unconscious in 1939 in *Moses and Monotheism*.[163] He mentioned the difficulties of transposing concepts from individual psychology to mass psychology. He considered the concept of collective unconscious to be ineffective, although, according to him, the unconscious is indeed collective but in the sense of a general property of human beings. Depth psychology certainly explains cultural facts and the mythological idea of the world is nothing other than a psychology projected into the external world. However, for Freud, neurosis is the model for thinking about the historical past of humanity and phylogenesis is approached with the categories of ontogenesis; the truth of myths lies in the figuration of human conflicts since the dawn of time. Whereas for Jung this historical past would explain not only neurosis but a psychic process belonging to the very nature of the human being, the expression of the development of the species, its obstacles and its resources.[164] The two approaches nevertheless partially overlap if we make neurosis this psychic process, but Jung would undoubtedly reject this identification of one with the other. For us, the common point is the exercise of the symbolic function and its vagaries. For Freud, moreover, the symbolic relationship, which the individual has never learned, can be rightly claimed as a phylogenetic heritage.[165] In *Moses and Monotheism*, he mentioned a transmission of a structural type, of a mode of operation identical to all humans which is quite close to Jung's position and his concept of archetype as the hereditary transmission of the capacity to evoke this or that element of the representative heritage.[166] But is it the capacity to evoke this or that element of the representative heritage or the *capacity of representation* itself, formed from "traces" with all the imprecision of this term? Freud mentioned, in this last writing, the phylogenetic transmission of mnemonic traces: "In my opinion there is an almost complete conformity in this respect between the individual and the group: in the group too an impression of the past is retained in unconscious memory-traces".[167]

The archaic heritage to which Freud refers in this text is that of the laws of language and symbolisation. It is that of relations between representations built in the course of the historical development of language and repeated at the individual level, but not only that. Archaic heritage of the human being encompasses not only dispositions but also mnemonic traces of what was experienced by previous generations:

> The behaviour of neurotic children towards their parents in the Oedipus and castration complex abounds in such reactions, which seem unjustified in the individual case and only become intelligible phylogenetically—by their connection with the experience of earlier generations. It would be well worth while to place this material, which I am able to appeal to here, before the public in a collected form. Its evidential value seems to me strong enough for me to venture on a further step and to posit the assertion that the archaic heritage of human beings comprises not only dispositions but also subject-matter—memory-traces of the experience of earlier generations.[168]

Freud's scruples about the reservations of biology about the transmission of acquired characteristics may now be overcome by current developments in epigenetics, but that is not the point. What do these memory traces consist of?: "After this discussion I have no hesitation in declaring that men have always known (in this special way) that they once possessed a primal father and killed him".[169] The transmission of these memory traces would therefore take place phylogenetically, through the unconscious, independently of direct communication. Jung could have said as much. These memory traces concern a very specific event, the murder of the father, a recurrent theme in the Freud–Jung relationship,[170] here in its inaugural place in collective history.

For Yerushalmi,[171] there is indeed a quasi-identity between the psychic life of the individual and that of the group in Freud. As early as his article *Obsessive Actions and Religious Practise* (1907), Freud characterises obsessional neurosis as individual religiosity and religion as a universal obsessional neurosis. He later added[172] that by adopting the universal neurosis, the individual is relieved of the task of developing a personal neurosis, a point of view that we are tempted to compare with Jung's concern with the avoidance of neurosis. For Freud, since *Totem and Taboo*, if the individual neurosis results from a repressed infantile trauma, this must also be the case for religion. Its origin lies in the murder of the primitive father and the repression of this act, the appearance of unconscious remorse and the subsequent institution of a father cult, in particular in the form of the totem animal and the totemic meal. This position is maintained and clarified in *Moses and Monotheism*:

> A tradition that was based only on communication could not lead to the compulsive character that attaches to religious phenomena. It would be

listened to, judged, and perhaps dismissed, like any other piece of information from outside; it would never attain the privilege of being liberated from the constraint of logical thought. It must have undergone the fate of being repressed, the condition of lingering in the unconscious, before it is able to display such powerful effects on its return, to bring the masses under its spell, as we have seen with astonishment and hitherto without comprehension in the case of religious tradition.[173]

In polytheism, the primitive Father, put to death by his sons, is forgotten. His memory is repressed or foreclosed and returns in monotheism. The murder of Moses, since this is Freud's hypothesis, is the repetition of this original murder where the act takes the place of the memory.[174] After a new period of latency, we witness the return of the Mosaic religion in the consciousness of the Jewish people. The Jews would have killed the father like the Christians, but they would not have admitted it. It is the sacrifice of Christ that would redeem the fault of the latter.

According to Yerushalmi, the obedience to the father afterwards, which came out of *Totem and Taboo*, would finally be realised through the writing of the text *Moses and Monotheism*, a text which, in a way, welcomed the return of the repressed contents, but which also made it possible thanks to the intervention of the supposedly historical truth, to preserve his independence of mind. Freud's position on Judaism in public would have been quite different from his private position. He would have received a much more extensive religious education than he claimed. This is evidenced by Jacob Freud's gift to his son on his 35th birthday in 1891 of his childhood Bible. It had been freshly bound and Jacob's dedication consisted of a "mosaic" of fragments and phrases from the Bible (*melitzah*), urging him to read the text again. In the *melitzah,* each word refers to the context from which it is taken. One cannot help but be struck by the analogy of this process with that of dreams.[175] Judaism and Christianity are both sons of God. Freud is a Jew without God and psychoanalysis is a Judaism without God. Yet psychoanalysis retains its fundamental monotheistic characteristics, but which ones? The religious? The relationship with the father? Freud–Jung: the same refusal of religion? Of the father? Or, of the religion of the father, even of the Father of the father? But not in the same way.

Notes

1 C. G. Jung, *"My life"*, *Memories, dreams, thoughts,* Paris, Gallimard, 1973.
2 C.G. Jung, *Freud's Theory on Hysteria: A Reply to Aschaffenburg,* Collected Works Vol. 4, Bollingen series/Princeton University Press (1953–1979).
3 H. Ellenberger, *Histoire de la découverte de l'inconscient,* Paris, Fayard, 1994.
4 C.G Jung, *On the Psychology of Dementia praecox* (1907) in Collected Works, *op. cit.*, Vol.3.

2
62 The Freud–Jung debate on symbols

5 J. Breuer and S. Freud, On the Psychical Mechanisms of Hysterical Phenomena (1893) in *The Standard Edition of the Complete Psychological Works of Sigmund Freud*, London, Hogarth Press (1953–1974), Vol. II.
6 S. Freud, The Neuro-psychoses of Defence (1895) in *SE*, Vol.III.
7 S. Freud, Psychopathology of Daily Life (1901), *SE*, Vol. VI.
8 *The Freud–Jung Letters* (1906–1914), ed.W.Mc Guire, Princeton University Press, 1974, Letter from Jung of 29.12.1906.
9 On the contrary, in our opinion, it is the existence of a common *but unelucidated* trait that commands the formation of the symbol. This common feature does not exclude differences in other respects.
10 C.G. Jung, *op. cit.*
11 C.G. Jung, *op. cit.*
12 C.G. Jung, *On the Psychogenesis of Schizophrenia* (1939), *Ibid.*
13 C.G. Jung, *Schizophrenia* (1958), *Ibid.*
14 C.G. Jung, Symbols of transformation, in *Collected works, op. cit.* Vol V.
     Symbols of transformation is the current title of the book. The title of the book was changed, for the first time, following Jung's break with Freud, replacing the word "libido" with the word "soul".
15 Jung would, much later, devote a study to the Book of Job.
16 It should be noted that at that time, for Jung, God was a substitute for the father.
17 This is an important point on which Jung rightly places great emphasis. Jung's God is a "psychological" God. It is a universal ingredient of the human psyche, an instance of sorts.
18 Honneger presented the Schwyzer case that Jung had entrusted to him at the Munich Congress.
19 *Symbols of transformations, op. cit.* A pipe hangs from the sun; the wind comes from it.
20 *Ibid.*
21 *Ibid.*
22 *Ibid.*
23 For Jung, it is not the father (but which father?) who blocks incest. On the contrary, he must be fought so that regression can happen and archetypal patterns can be put in place. They are "the father", the symbolic father, that of the prohibition of incest. It is this symbolic father that regression aims at, which must not be hindered by a father that could be called real.
     Jung's personal history supports this scenario, as his father probably did not manifest himself very much, which put Jung on another path of "symbolic" quest. We see here the ferment of what could not be elaborated from the transference to Freud at the time of the rupture between them, Jung being unable to assimilate Freud's excessive authority. On this subject, please refer to our book: *Le cas Jung, Aperçu sur la face psychotique du transference*, Paris, Anthropos Economica, 2017.
24 C.G. Jung, *The Red Book*, Liber Novus, S.Shamdasani (ed.), Philemon series & W.W. Norton & Co, 2009
25 The disappearance of the reality of the world, in schizophrenia, leaves this imaginary world with obvious archaic features. When a recent system disappears, a primitive, older system, takes its place. In neurosis, it is a fantasy of individual scope that replaces it. In schizophrenia, the loss of reality is compensated for by an older mode of adaptation, by archaic substitutes
26 *The Red Book* demontrates the implementatrion of this process in Jung himself.
27 Cl. Lévi-Strauss, "L'efficacité symbolique" in *Anthropologie structurale,* Paris, Plon, 1974.

28 *The Freud–Jung Letters*, ed.W. Mc Guire, Princeton University Press, 1974
29 Letter 17J, 31.03.1906.
30 Letter 22F, ca. 14–21.04.1907.
31 Letter 23F, 21.04.1907.
32 This remark makes it possible to grasp how the dream, which presupposes the libidinal investment of a representation, allows for the internalisation and sub-jectivisation of a representation previously present in delusion.
33 Not much is known about this attack. According to D. Bair (author of *Jung, a biography,* Boston, Little Brown & Company, 2003) it could be the work of a priest and friend of Jung's father.
34 Letter 49J, 28.10.07.
35 Letter 50J, 2.11.07.
36 Letter 72J, 20.02.08.
37 Letter 76F, 3.03.08.
38 Letter 99F, 21.06.08.
39 Letter 106F, 13.08.1908.
40 Letter 117J, 3.12.08.
41 *The significance of the father for the destiny of the individual* (1909), Collected works, Vol.4.
42 Letter 138J, 2.04.09.
43 Letter 170J, 25.12.09.
44 Letter 175J, 30.01.10.
45 Letter 177F, 2.02.1910.
46 Letter 169F, 19.12.1910.
47 Letter 181J, 2.03.10.
48 This lecture served as the matrix for his later work, *Metamorphoses of the Libido and its Symbols.*
49 Letter199F, 19.06.1910.
50 Letter 205F, 10.08.1910.
51 S. Freud, The Schreber case (1911), SE, Vol.XII.
52 Letter 218 F, 31.10.10.
53 Let us note, however, the mechanism behind these identifications: when a man (or woman) dies, his or her spiritual parts (nerves) undergo a process of purifi-cation in order to finally be integrated into God, and to constitute a part of Him, such as the vestibules (or forecourts) of heaven. In the course of this purification, souls learn the language spoken by God Himself, the "basic" language, which is rich in euphemisms.
54 Letter 241F, 14.03.1911.
55 Letter 243J, 19.03.191 1.
56 Freud's contribution was published in the Jarhbuch, III, 2 (*The Freud–Jung Letters, op.cit.*)
57 Letter 282 J, 14.11.11.
58 Letter 286 F, 30.11.11.
59 Letter 287J, 11.12.11.
60 Letter 303J, 3.03.1912.
61 Letter 315J, 17.05.12
62 Letter 316F, 23.05.1912
63 Letter 321J, 02.08.12.
64 Letter 323J, 11.11.12.
65 This is not exactly the case. The *Metamorphoses,* as we have seen, exposes the displacement of the sexual to the religious, in the Jungian sense, which is, it is true, considered superior.

The Freud–Jung debate on symbols

66 S. Freud, *On the History of the Psychoanalytic movement* (1914), SE, Vol.XIV. The Freud–Jung divide, one reasoning from neurosis and the other from psychosis, takes shape here.
67 Letter 329 F, 29.11.12.
68 Letter 342 F, 03.01.13.
69 Letter 355.J, 29.07.13. We agree with this remark.
70 Letter 357J, 27.10.13.
71 Jung was going through a major personal crisis from which the writing of *The Red Book* would enable him to emerge.
72 S. Freud, *On the History of the Psychoanalytic Movement, op. cit.*
73 This is an essential point. If analysis cannot elucidate the present without bringing it back to the past, the connection with the past is often not sufficient to eradicate its pressure, as repetition shows.
74 *On Narcissism: an introduction,* SE, vol.XIV, *op. cit.*
75 Ideal-Ego and Ego-ideal are not distinguished by Freud at this stage. The passage from one to the other requires a trait of the object erected as an ideal.
76 S. Spielrein, Destruction as the cause of coming into being, in *Journal of Analytical Psychology*, 1994, 39.
77 *Ibid.*
78 *Ibid.*
79 "The psychological content of a case of schizophrenia" in *A Secret Symmetry, Sabina Spielrein Between Jung and Freud*, Pantheon books, 1984.
80 It is this very matrix that Jung elaborates in his theory of archetypes.
81 Letter from Sabina Spielrein to Jung of 27–28 January 1918, *Ibid.*
82 S. Freud, *Introductory Lectures to Psychoanalysis*, SE, Vol. XV.
83 This term was introduced by Rudolph Otto, (from Latin, numen: deity) in *The Idea of the Holy,* Oxford University Press, 1923. Jung uses it to qualify a dynamic existence or effect which does not find its cause in an arbitrary act of the will. The adjective "religious" or "numinous" will thus designate for him the particular attitude of a consciousness that has been affected by the experience of the numinosum, in other words, by the experience of the unconscious.
84 C.G. Jung, *C.G. Jung speaking: Interviews and Encounters,* Princeton University Press, 1977.
85 C. G. Jung, The Conquest of Consciousness (1934) in *Collected Works*, Vol. 8.
86 Underlined by us. For Jung, transference, in its infantile and personal form, is the first phase of transference followed by another modality of transference of a collective nature seen mainly in the mobilisation of archetypes in dreams. We see this second phase, more distant from parental projections, as being closer to the Lacanian notion of analysing transference.
87 C.G. Jung, On the Psychology of the Unconscious, *Collected works*, Vol.7.
88 Although, perhaps not so contingent, like the role of the diurnal rest in Freud. In Jung's case, this contingent motif emerges from what he sees as the individual unconscious.
89 C.G. Jung, Psychology and Religion, *Collected works*, Vol.11.
90 D.Boukhabza, *La lettre du rêve, un lecteur por la psychose* (The dream letter: a reader for psychosis), érès/Arcanes, 2012.
91 The Houston films, interviews with C.G. Jung by Richard Evans, in *C.G. Jung speaks, op. cit.*
92 In the experience reported in *The Red Book*, it is a question of wresting the Self from God. This experience, which will be discussed later, is the origin of what Jung calls the individuation process: the inscription of the subject in the collective. Furthermore, it is a "direct" inscription which bypasses the symptom.

93 "Ordinary" madness is identified with the unconscious. Identification with the unconscious is the mark of madness as alienation. It is to be distinguished from "divine" madness, the path that Jung himself takes in *The Red Book*. This path is traced by a modification of the figure of God, producing a new God, who, when faced with the antagonism of opposites, seeks conciliation and reunion, and takes the form of the symbol. It is necessary to maintain the confrontation of the unconscious with its opposite to maintain the tension between the timeless, another name for the unconscious, and the actual.

94 C.G. Jung. *Commentary on the Mystery of the Golden Flower,* Psychology and religion, *op. cit.*

95 D. Boukhabza, *Le cas Jung, Aperçu sur la face psychotique du transfert* (The Jung Case: a Glimpse of the Psychotic Side of Transference), Paris, Anthropos/ Economica, 2017.

96 *Ibid.*

97 C. Maillard, *Au cœur du Livre rouge, Les Sept sermons aux morts (At the Heart of The Red Book: the Seven Sermons to the Dead)* Paris, Éditions Imago, La compagnie du Livre Rouge, 2017. Translated by us.

98 *Psychology and Religion, op.cit.*

99 *Ibid.*

100 Jean-Michel Rey, "L'universel que l'on dit chrétien" (The Universal Said to be Christian), *Universel et diversité, Insistance*, 8, érès, 2013.

101 *The Seven Sermons to the Dead* is the last part of *The Red Book*, first published separately from the rest before the entire *Red Book* was published. In the *Seven Sermons*, Basilides the Gnostic addresses a speech to the dead using the voice of Philemon, one of the symbols of *The Red Book*.

102 C. Maillard, *op.cit.*

103 The *principium individuationis* is a concept taken from Schopenhauer who defines time and space as the *principium individuationis*. It is what makes multiplicity possible. For Jung, it is the process of formation of the psychological individual as a being distinct from collective psychology, which is rendered by the term "individuation process".

104 C. Maillard, *ibid.*

105 The negative theology of Master Eckhart develops the idea of the relativity of the divine, associating God and Creature. A God with attributes cannot be absolute. It is this attribution of "qualities" (or "traits" in our own terminology) to God, derived from the notion of the Pleroma, that allows him to be related to the Creature and to be a decomposed instance i.e. the matrix of the symbol.

106 The crisis that gave rise to the writing of *The Red Book* was preceded by a period of recurring dreams around the theme of the awakening of the dead where the dead came back to life (*Le cas Jung*).

107 C. Maillard, *ibid.* This concept of polytheism finds one of its sources in Nietzche's *The Gay Science* (On the Greatest Utility of Polytheism).

108 *Ibid.*

109 *General aspects of dream psychology* (1928) in Collected Works, Vol.8.

110 *Ibid.*

111 Letter of 24 October 1912 in Lydia Marinelli and Andreas Mayer. *Dreaming by the Book: Freud's The Interpretation of Dreams and the History of Psychoanalysis,* New York, Other Press, 2003.

112 Silberer was one of Freud's first disciples from 1907 and a member of the Wednesday Circle from 1910 until his death by suicide in 1923. He developed a personal way of thinking around symbols and dreams. The starting point was the experiment he carried out on himself during the period of somnolence. He

observed the transformation of mental processes into images and based his anagogical and symbolic interpretation of dreams on these observations. The conditions favouring the formation of symbols are met when there is a movement towards or away from an idea. Silberer sees, following Wundt, the cause of the formation of symbols in the lack of apperception that characterises dreams. The symbol represents a shift from the intellect to the senses, and from the idea to the image. It is an attempt to represent something that escapes thought, and constitutes a way of approaching it, looking to the future as much as to the past.

113 *General aspects of dream psychology, op. cit.*
114 Christine Maillard, "Herbert Silberer (1882–1923). Genèse et enjeux d'une théorie de l'Alchimie" in *Recherches germaniques,* hors-série no 9, Strasbourg, 2014.
115 *General aspects of dream psychology, op. cit.*
116 This is also what Lévi-Strauss describes in "L'efficacité symbolique".
117 It is this succession of symbols with its energetic mobilisation that is the principle of the therapeutic dynamic; this dynamic is at play in the series of dreams underlying the individuation process.
118 The Tavistock lectures (1935) *Collected Works*, Vol. 18.
119 This term will be taken up in a similar sense, particularly in *Mille Plateaux (A Thousand plateaus)*, by the philosopher Deleuze and the psychiatrist Guattari who regularly refer to Jung.
120 C.G. Jung, *Psychology and Religion, op. cit.*
121 *Ibid.*
122 C.G. Jung, Psychology and Alchemy, *Collected Works*, Vol. 12.
123 These are lectures given by Jung at Yale in 1936 on the theme of psychology and religion.
124 The unity in question is quite provisional. It is that of the symbol that reconciles opposites.
125 *Ibid.*
126 *Ibid.*
127 The mandala designates the sacred circle used in Lamaism (Tibetan Buddhism). According to Lamaism, the mandala is an inner image, gradually constructed by the imagination at times when the psychic balance is disturbed or when a thought is missing and must be sought because it is not already contained in the sacred doctrine.
128 This ties in with our own clinical experience, as developed in *La lettre du rêve, op. cit.*
129 S. Freud, *The Interpretation of Dreams,* SE Vol.IV-V.
130 S.Freud, *Introductory Lessons to Psychoanalysis*, SE.Vol.XV-XVI.
131 The question arises, however, whether the latent elements at the origin of the dream are thoughts or whether they are rather, as we believe, pre-thoughts not yet articulated appearing through images and serving as an intermediary link in the subsequent elaboration of thought.
132 *The Freud–Jung Letters, op. cit,* Letter 181J.
133 J. Laplanche, *Problématiques II, castration-symbolisations,* Paris, PUF Quadrige, 1998.
134 S. Freud, *The Interpretation of Dreams, op. cit.*
135 J. Forrester, *Language and the Origins of Psychoanalysis,* MacMillan Press, 1980. According to Forrester, Freud accepted the idea of using universal symbolism only reluctantly and under pressure from the colleagues of his group at the time, both in Vienna (especially Stekel) and Zurich.

136 S. Freud. *Introductory Lectures on Psychoanalysis, part I and II*, SE. Vol.XV.
137 M. Arrivé, *Le concept de symbole en sémio-linguistique et en psychanalyse, Deuxième partie: Le symbole dans le texte de Freud* (The Concept of Symbol in Semio-linguistics and Psychoanalysis, Part 2, The symbol in Freud' works), Besançon, CNRS, 1981.
138 Underlined by us.
139 S. Freud, *Introductory Lectures on Psychoanalysis, op. cit.*
140 *Ibid.*
141 *The Interpretation of Dreams, op. cit.*
142 S. Freud, *The Antithetical Meanings of Primal Words*, SE Vol.XI.
143 *Ibid.*
144 Underlined by us.
145 S. Freud. *The Neuro-psychoses of defence (1894), op. cit.*
146 S. Freud, *The Aetiology of Hysteria* (1896) in SE Vol.3, *op. cit.*
147 Let us recall that the trace constitutes for Freud the condition of possibility of conservation and transfer of the excitation. (*The Interpretation of Dreams, op. cit.*)
148 S. Freud, *The Aetiology of Hysteria, op. cit.*
149 S. Freud, *Inhibition, Symptom and Anxiety*, SE Vol.XX.
150 *Ibid.*
151 Underlined by us.
152 *Ibid.*
153 M. Arrivé, *Le symbole dans le texte de Freud, op. cit.*
154 *The Interpretation of Dreams, op. cit.*
155 S.Freud. *Totem and Taboo* (1913), SE Vol.XIII.
156 As mentioned in the *Freud–Jung Letters*, the symbolic nature of the prohibition of incest and the value of regression was under debate between the two men at the time of Freud's writing of *Totem and Taboo*.
157 S. Freud, *Totem and Taboo*, SE Vol.XIII.
158 S. Freud, *Group Psychology and Analysis of the Ego* (1921) SE, Vol.XVIII.
159 In Jung's case, the murder will concern the hero. It is he who is murdered in the *Siegfried* dream at the beginning of the crisis (*Le cas Jung*). However, the heroic solution had already appeared in the *Metamorphoses of the Libido and its Symbols* in the form of Chiwantopel's fantasy, analysed by Miss Miller as that of a virile ideal—the residue of an identification with the father. It is this ideal that must fall, but this fall has to be accepted and it is the hero's sacrifice, deliberately consented to, that will open, in Jung's view, onto a *beyond of identification with the father*.
160 *The Ego and the Id*, in SE, Vol.XIX.
161 A single, unique trait that will become the unary trait in Lacan's seminar IX: Identification.
162 B. Karsenti, *L'homme total, Sociologie, anthropologie et philosophie chez Marcel Mauss (The Total Man: Sociology, Anthropology and Philosophy in Marcel Mauss' Works)*, Paris, puf, 2007.
163 S. Freud, *Moses and Monotheism*, SE, Vol.XXIII.
164 R. Barros Gewehr, "L'inconscient phylogénétique versus l'inconscient collectif: une contribution au dialogue entre Freud et Jung" (The phylogenetic unconscious versus the collective unconscious: a contribution to the dialogue between Freud and Jung), Revue de psychologie analytique, 2013, I, 1.
165 S. Freud, *Introductory Lectures on Psychoanalysis, op.cit.*
166 C.G. Jung, *Psychology of the Unconscious, op. cit.*
167 S. Freud, *Moses and Monotheism, op. cit.*

168 *Ibid.*
169 *Ibid.*
170 *Le cas Jung, op. cit.*
171 Y. H. Yerushalmi, *Freud's Moses, Judaïsm terminable et interminable*, Yale University Press, 1993.
172 S. Freud, *The Future of an Illusion* (1927), SE, Vol.XXI.
173 *Moses and Monotheism, op. cit.*
174 Let us recall that this is the Freudian concept of repetition compulsion.
175 In 1896, Jacob died. In 1900, the *Traumdeutung* was published.

Bibliography

Arrivé, M., *Le concept de symbole en sémio-linguistique et en psychanalyse, Deuxième partie: Le symbole dans le texte de Freud*, CNRS, Besançon, 1981.
Bair, D., *Jung, a biography*, Little Brown &Company, Boston, 2003.
Barros Gewehr, R., L'inconscient phylogénétique versus l'inconscient collectif, Contribution au dialogue entre Freud et Jung, *Revue de psychologie analytique*, 2013/1, 1.
Boukhabza, D., *La lettre du rêve, un lecteur pour la psychose*, érès/Arcanes, 2012.
Boukhabza, D., *Le cas Jung, Aperçu sur la face psychotique du transfert)*, Anthropos/Economica, Paris, 2017.
Breuer, J. and S. Freud, *On the Psychical Mecanisms of Hysterial Phenomena*, Vol. II, The Standard Edition of the Complete Psychological Works of Sigmund Freud, Hogarth Press, London, 1953–1974, 1893
Ellenberger, H., *Histoire de la découverte de l'inconscient*, Fayard, Paris, 1994.
Forrester, J., *Langage and the origins of psychoanalysis*, MacMillan Press, 1980.
Freud, S., *The neuro-psychoses of defence*, Vol. III, SE, 1895.
Freud, S., *The etiology of hysteria*, Vol. III, SE, 1896.
Freud, S., *The interpretation of dreams*, Vols. IV–V, SE, 1900.
Freud, S., *Psychopathology of daily life*, Vol. VI, SE, 1901.
Freud, S., *The antithetical meanings of primal words*, Vol. XI, SE, 1910.
Freud, S., *The case of Schreber*, Vol. XII, SE, 1911.
Freud, S., *Totem and taboo*, Vol. XIII, SE, 1913.
Freud, S., *On the history of the psychoanalytic movement*, Vol. XIV, SE, 1914.
Freud, S., *Introductory lectures to psychoanalysis*, Vols. XV–XVI, SE, 1915-1917.
Freud, S., *Group psychology and analysis of the ego*, Vol. 18, SE, 1921.
Freud, S., *The ego and the Id*, Vol. 19, SE, 1923.
Freud, S., *Inhibition, symptom and anxiety*, Vol. XX, SE, 1926.
Freud, S., *The future of an illusion*, Vol. XXI, SE, 1927.
Freud, S., *Moses and monotheism*, Vol. XXIII, SE, 1939.
Jung, C. G., *Freud's theory on hysteria: a reply to Aschaffenburg*, Vol. 4, Collected works.
Jung, C. G., *Psychology and religion*, Vol. 11, Collected works.
Jung, C. G., *Psychology of dementia praecox*, Collected works, Vol. 3., Bollingen series/Princeton University Press, 1953–1979, 1907.
Jung, C. G., *The significance of the father for the destiny of the individual*, Vol. 4, Collected works, 1909.
Jung, C. G., *Symbols of transformation*, Vol. V, Collected works, 1911-1912.

Jung, C. G., *On the psychology of the unconscious*, Vol. 8, Collected works, 1916.

Jung, C. G., *General aspects of dream psychology*, Vol. 8, Collected Works, 1928.

Jung, C. G., *The Tavistock lectures*, Vol. 18, Collected works, 1935.

Jung, C. G., *On the psychogenesis of schizophrenia*, Collected works, Vol. 3, 1939.

Jung, C. G., *Schizophrenia*, Collected works, Vol. 3, 1958.

Jung, C. G., *Memories, dreams, thoughts* (1961), Random House, 1965.

Jung, C. G., *C.G. Jung speaking: Interviews and encounters*, Princeton University Press, 1977.

Jung, C. G., *The Red Book*, Liber Novus, S. Shamdasani (ed.), Philemon Series & W.W. Norton & Co, 2009.

Karsenti, B., *L'homme total, Sociologie, anthropologie et philosophie chez Marcel Mauss*, puf, Paris, 2007.

Laplanche, J., *Problématiques II, castration-symbolisations*, PUF Quadrige, Paris, 1998.

Lévi-Strauss, C. l., *L'efficacité symbolique* in Anthropologie structurale, Plon, Paris, 1974.

Maillard, C., "Herbert Silberer ((1882–1923). Genèse et enjeux d'une théorie de l'Alchimie", in *Recherches germaniques*, hors-série no 9, Université de Strasbourg, Strasbourg, 2014.

Maillard, C., *Au cœur du Livre rouge, Les Sept sermons aux morts*, Éditions Imago, La compagnie du Livre Rouge, Paris, 2017.

Marinelli, L. and A. Mayer, *Dreaming by the book: Freud's The Interpretation of dreams and the history of psychoanalysis*, Other Press, NewYork, 2003.

The Freud-Jung Letters, ed. W. Mc Guire, Princeton University Press, 1974.

Otto, R., *The idea of the Holy*, Oxford University Press, 1923.

Yerushalmi, Y. H., *Freud's Moses, Judaïsm terminable et interminable*, Yale University Press, 1993.

Chapter 2

The symbolic function

From Mauss to Lévi-Strauss

The notion of "symbolic function" stems from French ethnology and above all, Marcel Mauss' research. The gift system[1] encompasses a large number of ancient societies, but equally, it permeates our modern societies where it retains its effectiveness, through our laws and morality, as the principal form of the social bond. The archaic is of the order of the past, but a past that is always reactivated and involved in the present. Sociological observation of our own social life, insofar as it implies an unveiling of this oblivion, cannot be constructed directly.[2] It requires an external perspective. The encounter with otherness and the deciphering of its symbolic logic enables us to deduce our own. The archaeological method proves to be a specific practice which, far from considering the past as a relic, considers it as an ancient foundation whose effects, which are systematically forgotten, are felt in the present. The absence of the gift is significant in that it reveals a forgetting of the gift. The main characteristic of the archaic level, in a Maussian sense, is that it acts as an unconscious structural device that continually underlies the entirety of our social life and gives it its specific configuration. The oblivion of the gift has an essential function as a mark of the symbolic logic from which it proceeds, a logic that is properly unconscious, not simply in the sense that it is veiled but in the sense that the very veiling is the condition of its effectiveness. The similarities between past and present are not the result of the survival of a residue, but of a permanence whose real effects can be spotted despite the encryption.

The work of Mauss was taken up by Lévi-Strauss[3] who recognised the primacy of the symbolic function in societies. The mental and the social merging and their symbolic origin is what unites them. For Lévi-Strauss, the particular situation of the social sciences is due to the intrinsic character of its object being both object and subject, or thing and representation. The laws of unconscious activity are always outside subjective apprehension, yet they determine themselves the modalities of this apprehension; we can become aware of them but only as an object. Does a society derive its institutional

DOI: 10.4324/b23380-3

characteristics from the distinctive features of the personality of its members, or is this personality explained by early childhood education, which are themselves cultural phenomena? The psychological formulation is merely a translation, on the level of the individual psyche, of a structure that is already properly sociological.

It is in the nature of society that it expresses itself symbolically in its customs and institutions; on the contrary, normal individual behaviours are *never symbolic in themselves*. They are elements from which a symbolic system, which can only be collective, is constructed. It is only the abnormal behaviours which, because they are de-socialised and in a way abandoned to themselves, create the illusion of an autonomous symbolism on an individual level.[4]

For Lévi-Strauss, therefore, it is the primacy of the symbolic function that founds the unity of the mental and the social. The individual and the social are in a relationship of translation: they can be considered as the differentiated expressions of the same signifying framework. Mauss, with the notion of mana, attempted to reach a sort of fourth dimension—a plane on which the notions of unconscious category and collective category would merge. It is *above the distinction between the individual and the collective* that the unconscious stands, as the mediating term between the self and the other. It is an operation of the same type which, in psychoanalysis, allows us to reclaim for ourselves our most foreign self, and, in ethnological investigation, gives us access to the most foreign of the others as to "another us".[5]

Thus, the magical judgement in the act of producing smoke to bring about rain, for example, is based on the fact that, at a so-called deeper level, thought identifies smoke and cloud and that this identification justifies the association. Magical operations are based on the restoration of an unconscious unity or perhaps, rather, an unconscious identification. In his 1949 article *L'efficacité symbolique*, Lévi-Strauss posits the equivalence between shamanic and psychoanalytic cures, but with an inversion of the terms:

The shaman has the same dual role as the psychoanalyst—a first role of listener for the psychoanalyst, and of speaker for the shaman. He builds an immediate relation with the consciousness (an a mediated one with the unconscious) of the patient[...] The patient suffering from neurosis puts an end to an individual myth by opposing a real psychoanalyst; the indigenous woman who has just given birth overcomes a genuine organic disorder by identifying with a mythically transposed shaman [...] In fact the shamanic cure seems to be an exact equivalent of the psychoanalytic cure, but with an inversion of all terms. Both aim to provoke an experience; and both achieve this by reconstructing a myth that the patient must live, or relive. But in the one case, it is an individual myth that the patient builds with the help of elements drawn from his past; in the other case it is a social myth, which the patient receives from the outside, and which does not correspond to a previous personal state.[6]

The myth: construction of the drive trait

If the psychic life of the individual and that of the group are organised in an identical way, what are the supports? Lévi-Strauss proceeds from an examination of collective thought and identifies the way in which myth is constructed through the identification of a group with an animal *via* this or that trait. This trait comes from the instinctual life, like orality in *La Potière jalouse*[7]. It brings about a relationship—a connection between distinct semantic fields—between a creative activity such as pottery (producing a container) with jealousy (an avatar of an overflowing orality), after a whole series of transformations.

Indeed, as Lévi-Strauss confirms, the raw material elaborated by the myth is derived from the instinctual life and its avatars. The successive steps of this elaboration, relating here to orality and anality, are developed in *La Potière jalouse*. This link of the myth to the drive, the drive of the body, is the great absentee of Jungian thought, which refers only to the products of the transformation of this material in spheres other than those of the body. Lévi-Strauss shows these drive transformations from the sphere of the body to other fields. He highlights the role of the *trait*, on which the identification of a group with a particular animal is based. A clan believes that there is a physical or moral resemblance with its eponymous animal, for example. This is Freud's starting point in *Totem and Taboo*. The trait of resemblance can be considered the product of a genealogical transmission. For example, certain Latin American tribe thinks it is descended from a certain animal ancestor of which it possesses a certain characteristic trait. The traits selected are from the realm of sensory experience, character traits or moral values, or even make the transition from one to the other, belonging to both the natural and the social world.

Lévi-Strauss' analysis takes into account the various versions of this myth connecting pottery and jealousy, with the understanding that all of them constitute the one he is dealing with. This one involves a bird, the Nightjar and its characteristics. The mythology of South-East Asia places great importance on the Nightjar as a blacksmith bird and a servant of thunder, but also as a rice-growing bird and producer of good crops. *An oral trait* is given to it; it is called by a name which means "eating to satiety". The Nightjar is variously named in different languages, but these names all refer to the bird's huge mouth, which allows it to gobble up enormous prey. It is considered by some people to be a reincarnation of the spirit of the dead.

The Nightjar is also present in South American mythology where it is associated with the origin of pottery. In one of the versions, Sun and Moon, back then humans, live on the earth and have the same wife, Aôho. The latter shows a preference for the sun; the moon then takes offence and climbs into the sky with the help of a vine. Then, by blowing on the sun, the moon eclipses it. Aôho, feeling abandoned, follows the moon into the sky carrying a basket of pottery clay. The moon, who wants to get rid of her for good, cuts the vine which linked the two worlds. Aôho falls with her basket, spilling the clay onto the earth. She then changes into a Nightjar. The sun then climbs into the sky, using another vine, but the moon continues to flee; they will never travel together. Because the stars were jealous of each other and fought over a woman, the Jivaros never cease to be jealous of each other nor to fight for her. According to another myth from a tribe close to the Jivaros, the pottery clay comes from the excrement of the Nightjar woman. This excrement is linked, by a series of other versions of the myth, to the theme of formlessness already present in the first myth through the element of "vine". The work of pottery consists precisely in giving form to this shapeless material that constitutes the pottery clay. But we must add something else: the shaping is also connected to the theme of representation and that of "holding", specific to the work of symbolisation. The shape/shapeless opposition is thus worked on by the myth, as is the opposition between the levels of the universe, heaven and earth, through the circulation of the protagonists between these two levels.

But the Nightjar is also linked to jealousy. Another myth tells the story of how, one night, the elder of two sisters admired the evening star. The next day, the star entered her hut in the form of a stooped old man who asked her to marry him. The elder sister, horrified, refused but her younger sister, moved by pity, accepted. The following day, it is revealed that the old man's body concealed a handsome young man, who was also gifted with talents unknown to the Indians. Jealous and ashamed, the eldest sister turned into a Nightjar. Let us note here the occurrence of the figure of metamorphosis, redundant in myths as in dreams. Orality is also present in myths in which the Nightjar occupies a central place and is expressed against a background of excessive attachment to maternal nourishment. This attachment, this oral fixation, also constitutes the impulse material on which the transformation, the destiny of the impulse that constitutes jealousy here, was built.

However, Levi-Strauss needs to also establish the link between pottery and the Nightjar. He must resort then to another term, another bird, which has no place in the preceding myths. Nevertheless, on the one hand, this bird is present in other myths that are logically and geographically linked to those of the Nightjar, and on the other hand, the habits of this bird are diametrically opposed to those of the Nightjar. While the latter is associated with myths about separation or estrangement of the sexes, the Hornero, as the bird is called, is a symbol of marital harmony. As much as the Nightjar is greedy and gluttonous, the Hornero is altruistic and nurturing. The perfection of its nest, resembling a termite mound, attracts attention. Finally, the Hornero is attributed a role of transmission of *savoir faire*. He is said to have taught the art of building houses and making pottery to the ancestors of another tribe. So much so that we are led to see in the Hornero an "inverted Nightjar", or a Nightjar -1. Here, we apply a principle of myth analysis, equally valid for dream analysis, which says that a symbol and its opposite are one and the same. It can be used in one direction or in the opposite direction. It connotes the same tendency, the same impulse motion, which can be reversed; this is a major characteristic of the drive. The transformations of the myth thus lead to an equivalence which Levi-Strauss writes as follows and which he calls the "canonical formula of myth" (formule canonique du mythe).

$$F_{jealousy}(\text{Nightjar}) : F_{potter}(\text{Female}) :: F_{jealousy}(\text{Female}) : F_{Nightjar-1}(\text{potter})$$

The Nightjar's "jealousy function" is to the woman's "pottery function" what the woman's "jealousy function" is to the pottery woman's "inverted Nightjar function". The use of the Hornero as a function, rather than a term, enables us to verify the system of equivalences. It transforms what was initially a transcendental deduction (that the Nightjar could be the origin of pottery) into an empirical one. In view of experience, the Hornero is a master potter, just as in view of experience, the Nightjar is a jealous bird. We could also go a little further, or at least on a more analytical path, and say that the pottery symbolises the limits or restraints brought to the oral drive, here *via* the Hornero, whose defect is transmuted into jealousy, which the Nightjar symbolises here. The dream of a Jivaro Indian in the grip of jealousy could represent the problematic. The myth thus poses a problem that its transformations try to solve and deal with, posing the analogy to one another

> [...] the object (of myth) derives its substance from the invariant properties that mythic thought manages to bring out when it *compares a plurality of statements*[8]. To make it simpler, we could say that myth is a system of logical operations defined by the method of "it is when ... " or "it is like ... ".[9]

Mythic reflection operates through several codes. Each one extracts properties from one domain of experience that allows it to be compared with other domains and to be translated into each other in the manner of a text that might be intelligible in one language but which, when rendered in several languages, would see its meaning broadened and deepened. "The message of myth rests on the property that all codes, as codes, are mutually convertible".[10] Indeed, in *The Jealous Potter,* Lévi-Strauss considers examining a family of myths in which the sexual code is involved, but only alongside other codes such as technological, zoological and cosmological ones. Let us pass over the fact that he would join Jung despite himself[11] to examine this question more closely. In myths, but also in dreams, we are dealing with a conversion of one code into another. The symbol is not a simple comparison. "The transfer of meaning does not take place from term to term but from code to code, from one class of terms to another one".[12] Lévi-Strauss takes up the example of Silberer quoted by Freud[13]: "I think I intend to improve a rough passage in my talk. Vision: I see myself polishing a piece of wood with a plane". It is not so much the passage from the abstract to the concrete that is important here, but rather the relation of one to the other:

> When it (metaphor) replaces one with the other, terms belonging to different codes, it is based on the intuition that these terms, seen from above, connote the same semantic field: it is this semantic field that it reconstitutes notwithstanding the efforts of analytical thought to divide it[14]. The purpose of the metaphor, in this case the planer, is not so much to replace a term from a given class with another, from another class, but *to (re)connect one with the other.*

Dreams also connect two registers because of their recourse to the image—their function of a rebus. It is this recourse that gives dreams their value as an exemplary connecting tool that founds its effectiveness in the treatment of psychoses[15]. Can we reduce the "translation" from code to code that Lévi-Strauss mentions in his analysis of dreams to the reciprocal translation between representations of words and representations of things, as developed by Freud in *The Unconscious*[16]? This translation would realise the link uniting the treasure of language—the sediment with which human experience has charged language, a collective dimension of experience as it were—and the individual experience insofar as it is based on the *perceptum.* For the individual, it is the trace of perception that will be constituted as a representation of a thing in dreams, by means of the image, waiting to be linked to a representation of a word, resulting from the collective experience that works in language.

> To use a metaphor is to divert a word or a phrase from one syntagmatic chain to another syntagmatic chain. As for symbol, it constitutes an entity which, in a certain conceptual order, maintains the same syntagmatic relations with the context as, in another conceptual order, the thing symbolised maintains with another context. Symbolic thought thus places homologous terms in a paradigmatic relationship, each term being in a particular syntagmatic context.[17]

This is what happens when dreams are brought together. We then obtain series characterised by the recurrence of a certain number of signifiers. These signifiers, integrated each time into different sequences, not only make it possible to link the sequences together, but also to constitute themselves as the associative links, i.e. the paradigms of these syntagms. This is the spring of the metaphor that is broken in psychosis and that Jung, in his own way, comes to seek in the function of symbols whose role is to restore the link *from code to code*: from one semantic field to another semantic field. One issue concerns the univocal or equivocal meaning of symbols. For Freud, as for Jung, symbols combine these two aspects. Indeed, we cannot deny the existence of a collective symbolism which charges certain terms with a determined meaning, but this collective determinism is each time relativised by the singular use of the symbol through the context, which is illustrated by the different connections between symbols. We can make a parallel between the connection between symbols and the ways in which myth is transformed, as considered by Lévi-Strauss in his canonical formula. For Lévi-Strauss too, symbols only acquire meaning insofar as they establish relationships. The meaning of the symbol is only "positional".

Oedipus: the repetition of a trait

Myths are part of the world of language. Their meaning does not come from the isolated elements that make them up but from their connections to each other. However, myths have specific properties that function at a higher level than those found in language, namely, phonemes, morphemes and semanthemes. These units, which Lévi-Strauss calls "mythèmes", are assimilated to "packages of relations" whose combination has a signifying function. This system has two dimensions—diachronic and synchronic—in a relationship similar to what "language" is to "speech" and vice versa. In *Structural Anthropology*,[18] Lévi-Strauss applies these considerations to the Oedipus myth. The Freudian Oedipus is conceived as a version of the myth of which all versions should be interpreted together. Lévi-Strauss' analysis of the Oedipus myth also includes elements from previous versions of the myth than the one recounted in Sophocles' theatre. The myth that must be considered is the one that groups together all its versions rather than the "original" myth, as Freud, always preoccupied with the haunting question of origin, says in his *Correspondence* with Jung.

The diagram presented by Lévi-Strauss (Figure 2.1)[19] is centred on the transmission of a drive trait. All the relations grouped in the same column present a *common trait* that must be identified. It is this common trait which successive generations have to deal with and which underlies the inexorable repetition. Lévi-Strauss' analysis identifies this trait on two levels: that of its transformations and that of its distribution across generations. We deem it necessary to reproduce here the table drawn up in his work in order to better grasp the similarity between the distribution of the traits presented in Lévi-Strauss' schema and those that would be distributed according to series of dreams, as we shall see later.

Cadmus seeks
his sister Europe,
ravished by Zeus

                                                 Cadmus kills
                                                 the dragon

The Sappartoi
exterminate
each other

                                                                        Labdacus (father of
                                                                        Laius)= "lame"(?)

                          Oedipus kills his   Laius (father of
                          father Laius   Oedipus) =
                                                                        "awkward"(?)

                                      Oedipus
                                      immolates the
                                      sphinx

                                                                     Oedipus =
                                                                     "swollen foot" (?)

Oedipus marries
Jocasta, his mother

                          Eteocles kills his
                          brother
                          Polynices

Antigone buries
Polynices, her brother,
violating the ban

Figure 2.1 Structural Anthropology.

The first column groups blood relatives whose proximity is excessive, whether really incestuous or not (they are said to be "overestimated" by Lévi-Strauss). The common trait is incestuous proximity. The second column takes up the same theme in an inverted form, since it is about murders, with murder being considered here as the inverted trait of incestuous proximity. The third column, Lévi-Strauss tells us, concerns monsters and their destruction. It also has a connection (not mentioned by Lévi-Strauss) with the second column; it is also about murders, but this time of monstrous animals. The dragon is a chthonian monster that must be destroyed so that men can be born from the earth. Both monsters refer to man's autochthony, the fact of being born from the earth. Since the monsters are ultimately defeated, the common feature retained here by Lévi-Strauss is the negation of man's autochthony.

The fourth column contains proper names, each of which, in its own way, connotes the difficulty of walking upright. Men born of the earth are often represented, at the time of emergence, as still unable to walk. *The common feature of the fourth column would therefore refer to the persistence of human autochthony*, i.e. the inversion of the feature of the third column.

The myth would thus read, in its own way, the alternative between a birth from the earth, an autochthony, and its opposite, that is, as Lévi-Strauss tells us, a bisexual reproduction. The myth therefore poses the question: is one born of one or of two?

By systematically applying this method of structural analysis, we manage to order all the known variants of a myth into a *series*[20], forming a sort of group of permutations, and where the variants placed at the two ends of the series offer a symmetrical but inverted structure in relation to each other. We thus introduce the beginnings of order where everything was chaos, and we gain the additional advantage of releasing certain logical operations, which are at the basis of mythical thought.[21]

Myth is taken by Lévi-Strauss as a kind of tool capable of mediating between contradictory terms; in the Oedipal example, between, on the one hand, the belief in man's autochthony (attested to in the myths of emergence concerning Mother Earth), and on the other, birth through the union of a man and a woman (as required by the social code of filiation). Mythical language functions as a kind of concatenation of exceptional signifiers, as we shall see later, allowing symbolic thought to be exercised. Among other things, mythical thought becomes aware of oppositions and tends to progressively mediate them. It proceeds from the analysis of a pair of opposites, of opposing traits, whose tension is resolved through the variants of this myth, ordering thought.

What interests us in this analysis of the Oedipus myth by Levi-Strauss is the emphasis on the trait in the elaboration of the different versions of the myth. The trait "overestimation" and its opposite "murder" index, in an opposite way, the incestuous problematic, just as the trait "murder of a monster" and "difficulty in walking straight" index the problematic of being born of the earth (rather than of two). A further step would link incest and the birth of two as a pair of opposites. The transmission, through generations, of a symbolic distortion is conveyed by the trait via the myth in the collective and via the symbol in the individual.

In the individual, dreams proceed in the same way. The trait and its opposite are the elements forming a dialectical couple whose essential function is the confrontation of a pair of opposites. This confrontation of opposites is the condition for the advent of the signifier. The Jungian definition of the symbol, seen from this viewpoint, is similar to that of the signifier. However, in Jung's thinking the role of the symbol is the linking of *a pair of opposites* but does the linkage leave any residue? The succession of symbols, which for Jung is connected to the process of individuation, shows that individuation is dependent on a succession. The signifiers are always associated, whereas symbols can remain alone, condensing several meanings, at least two of which are contradictory. However, under the impulse of transference, the symbols do not remain alone, but become associated. It is the process of association of symbols *via* the dream that Jung calls the individuation process. Symbols have a signifying value. Their function, as in Lévi-Strauss' mythical thought, is to mediate an opposition and in so doing, to tie up dissociated, cleaved signifying chains; it is to create this link from one semantic field to another allowing the circulation of meaning. In myths, the collective prevails. The individual is erased while being included, and this is the basis of Jung's interest in myths and the trait that he emphasises. It is the identification with this trait, which is conveyed by the myth, that has, for Jung, the value of a unary trait. But, for him, the trait remains attached to the symbol and he is not aware of the repetition as repetition of the subject, and as a manifestation of the subject; the symbolic function is not named as such. However, it manifests in Jung's method of dream interpretation highlighting dream series. The analysis of these series produces meaning by relating recurrent elements each time to a renewed context whose motifs shed light on repetition just like the one that crosses generations in the schema produced by Lévi-Strauss.

Lacan: reader of Lévi-Strauss

Markos Zafiropoulos has done excellent work[22] attempting to integrate or reintegrate psychoanalysis into the social sciences as a whole through his revisiting of the symbolic function. For him, it is the social evolution of symbolic forms and the effects of subjectivisation that lead us to speak of symbolic function rather than paternal function. Zafiropoulos follows, step by step, the impact of this notion in Lacan's work and its dialogue, explicit or implicit, with Lévi-Strauss. For him, Lacan went through a "Durkheimian moment" (before 1950) resulting in a sociohistorical relativism of the subjective structuring[23]. Lacan's return to Freud should then be considered as a moment of mutation which takes into account Lévi-Strauss' version of the reign of the symbolic function, to the detriment of Durkheim's version of family life.

For Lacan, it is the symbolic integration of the subject that counts and the Oedipus complex is only one of the keys. The Oedipus complex is a symbolic situation among others. The symptom depends on the "social conditions of Oedipus" which makes the subject's maturation dependent on the paternal imago, which is directly correlated to the social value of the father of the family. This is not the Freudian position for which the Oedipus is universal and timeless. For Lacan, it is the symbolic function that is universal and it is "social evolution (that) reduces the prohibition of incest to the modest dimensions of the Oedipal drama".[24]

An individual myth

The notion of symbolic function will be taken up by Lacan, first of all in *Fonction de la psychanalyse en criminologie* (Function of Psychoanalysis in Criminology), to affirm, following Mauss, the symbolic character of social structures as well as to inscribe the specificity of the psychopathic act in them:

> So let us find again the clear formulas that Mauss's death brings back to the day of our attention; the structures of society are symbolic; the individual, as a normal person, uses them for real conducts; as a psychopath, he expresses them by symbolic conducts. But it is obvious that the symbolism thus expressed can only be fragmentary, at most it can be said that it signals the point of rupture that the individual occupies in the network of social aggregations.[25]

It is the way the family group is inserted into the social group and from the flaws in this insertion that the contours of the individual's psychopathological manifestations, in other words, the form of his or her symptom, will take shape.

The notion of "individual myth" was used by Lacan in 1953 in his article *Le mythe individuel du névrosé* (The Individual Myth of the Neurotic)[26] to introduce, based on Freud's *Rat Man*, the gap between the symbolic, the imaginary and the real in relation to the function of the father. The paternal complex is situated as the motor of resistance. If the work of resistance solicits the capacity to decipher, it is to find the living language of symbols. Still in 1953, the symbol is, for Lacan, at the heart of the paradoxical relationship between speech and language in the subject.[27] In psychosis, this relationship manifests itself in the form of a word that has renounced recognition. The symbols of the unconscious are present but in a form described as petrified. Lacan also indicates on this occasion the interest in identifying the place of these subjects in the social space as witnesses "of the effects of rupture produced by the symbolic disjunctions, characteristic of the complex structures of civilisation". These relationships are also manifested in neurosis, but in this case in the field of the symptom:

The symptom is here the signifier of a signified repressed from the subject's consciousness. A symbol written on the sand of the flesh and on the veil of Maia participating in language through the semantic ambiguity that we have already underlined in its constitution. But it is a full-fledged speech, because it includes the speech of the other in the secret of its cipher. Deciphering this speech, Freud found the primary language of symbols, still alive in the suffering of the man of civilisation (*Das Unbehagen in der Kultur*). Hieroglyphics of hysteria, blazons of phobia, labyrinths of *Zwangneurosis* [...], such are the hermetisms that our exegesis resolves, the equivocations that our invocation dissolves, liberating the imprisoned meaning, which goes from the revelation of the palimpsest to the given word of the mystery and the forgiveness of the word.[28]

In 1954, Lacan spoke at the Congress of Religious Psychology together with Laforgue and Mircea Eliade. Lacan declared that the symbol exists within its world of symbols, and it cannot exist on its own. The symbol only exists as such within a system. He gives the example of number.

[...] the number is the symbol par excellence. I'll tell you in passing, it's the only point where the signifier and the signified come together in such a curious way that they become, strictly speaking, indistinguishable.[29]

The following discussion pits Lacan against Eliade and focuses on the relationship of symbols to words and the place of the symptom. Eliade intervenes to say that in certain cultures, symbols do not duplicate words.

In the Ionian languages there is no expression for "being", nor for non-being, nor for "becoming", but there are symbolic norms, an ontology of being. Symbolism is a language, but it is not words that you have analysed so admirably. This kind of speech is directly symbols. The documents are even more precious, because there are images, the spiral for example. There is a symbolism linked to the spiral, the whole image of the spiral is *in nuce* a symbol of "becoming". So as an ethnologist, I think it's dangerous to equate, as you do so well, speech and symbolism. At a certain level of culture, articulated language has its function, but *symbolism precedes it.*[30]

Lacan's response:

... I did not say that speech and symbols were the same thing. I confuse them so little that I said that symbols, in the form in which we, psychoanalysts, see it embodied, have, in the speaking subject, the meaning of passive words.

And further on:

I said that, in the symptom, in the fact of the symptom, we can consider that man is spoken. In the symptom, man is not the agent of speech, that is what it means.

The symptom is a symbol through which man is spoken to, precisely where he cannot speak himself. If the symptom is underlain by speech, it is from a point where it cannot be uttered.[31]

These distinctions are essential for the subject at hand.

The mirror of the dream

During 1953–54, the mirror stage is re-read by Lacan alongside the symbolic function. This text constitutes, in a way, a reprise, in its Lacanian version, of Freud's article *Narcissism, an Introduction*. It shows how the structuring of the subject of the unconscious takes place at the junction of the imaginary and the symbolic. In the montage of the upside-down bouquet,[32] the eye symbolises the subject, but for the knotting to take place correctly *the eye must be suitably situated.*

> ... it is on the position that is made for the subject in the symbolic that he can get his bearings in the dialectic of the inside-outside tying the imaginary to the real (the image of the body to the real of desire or drive).[33]

Lacan himself indicated that he referred, for this montage, to *the instrument that serves psychic productions as a sort of complicated microscope that Freud summons in the Interpretation of Dreams.* Indeed, the transformation of thought into visual images that dreams achieve led Freud to the idea of a psychic place particular to dreams:

> I shall remain upon psychological ground, and I propose simply to follow the suggestion that we should picture the instrument which carries out our mental functions as resembling a compound microscope or a photographic apparatus, or something of the kind. On that basis, psychical locality will correspond to a point inside the apparatus at which one of the preliminary stages of an image comes into being. In the microscope and telescope, as we know, these occur in part at ideal points, regions in which no tangible component of the apparatus is situated [...] Accordingly, we will picture the mental apparatus as a compound instrument, to the components of which we will give the name of "agencies", or (for the sake of greater clarity) "systems". It is to be anticipated, in the next place, that these systems may perhaps stand in a regular spatial relation to one another, in the same kind of way in which the various systems of lenses in a telescope are arranged behind one another. Strictly speaking, there is no need for the

hypothesis that the psychical systems are actually arranged in a *spatial* order. It would be sufficient if a fixed order were established by the fact that in a given psychical process the excitation passes through the systems in a particular *temporal* sequence.[34]

This is how Freud introduced what became the Perception-Consciousness diagram showing the different systems through which excitation travels from its perceptive end (outside of memory) to its motor end, passing through three essential systems: the S-system or system of signs of perception, the unconscious system and the preconscious system. It is thus to the optical material that is the support, in Freud, of the Perception-Consciousness schema, an essential schema for the mechanism of dreams and regression, that Lacan refers for his montage of the inverted bouquet.

Lacan later indicated[35] an additional element. In order to see oneself properly in the mirror the relation to the totem, i.e. to the dead father, i.e. to the Superego and the Ego-ideal, must be *internalised*. This passage from the outside to the inside is achieved by the introjection of the Superego via the totemic meal. It is the dialectic of introjection that produces the turn from the Superego (external) to the Ego-ideal (internal) and is thus sufficiently *narcissised* to constitute an object of libidinal investment for the ego. Primordial identification is understood as identification with a trait of the object, with a sign[36] that comes from the Other, towards whom the subject in the mirror turns to be sure of who he is. How does the subject internalise the gaze of the Other? It is interiorised by a sign of the Other's assent: a single trait. It is enough for the subject to coincide with this sign in the mirror, and in the relationship with the Other, so that he can dispose of this sign. This movement could also be the one from which the transference comes and the mooring point of the latter, particularly in the field of psychoses. *In fact, it is the symbolic function itself, of which the Ego Ideal is only one of the avatars, that must be internalised* and it is the function of dreams to carry out this introjection, through different mechanisms.

Symbols introduce, in fact, a third party. The subject is led to see himself in a series of images, or symbols, which depend on the symbolic circumstances that have organised his history. The stability of the image of the ego depends on the stability of the symbolic relations regulating it, and the history of its narcissistic capture makes it possible to perceive what were the symbolic circumstances of the subject. Indeed, the subject of the symptom is the subject of a symbolic universe whose laws he does not know. This is what is at stake in the analysis of the Rat Man, where this "ignorance" constantly brings the son's symptom back to the father's fault. The symbolic function includes "but overclasses—generically as well as clinically—the Oedipus complex in the process of constitution of the subject and of the unconscious messages organising his symptoms".[37] It is this generic and clinical over-classification that will form the basis of Lacan's further elaboration of the Name-of-the-Father function, partially taking up the notion of mana, as was described by Mauss, and linking the category of the unconscious with that of the collective, then re-elaborated by Lévi-Strauss, getting closer to linguistics.

Mana and the Name-of-the-Father

... we see in mana, wakan, orenda and other such notions the conscious expression of a semantic function, the role of which is to enable symbolic thought to be exercised despite the contradiction that is inherent in it. This explains the seemingly insoluble antinomies attached to this notion, which have so struck ethnographers and which Mauss has highlighted: force and action; quality and state; noun and adjective and verb at the same time; abstract and concrete; omnipresent and localised. And indeed, mana is all these things at once; but isn't it precisely because it is none of these things: a simple form, or more exactly, a symbol in its pure state, and therefore capable of taking on any symbolic content? In this system of symbols that constitutes all cosmology, it would simply be a *zero symbolic value*, that is to say, a sign marking the necessity of an additional content to the one that the signified holds already, which can be any value provided by the available reserve, and which is not, as phonologists say, a group term.[38]

And Lévi-Strauss specifies, in a footnote, this connection with linguistics by quoting Jakobson and his definition of the zero phoneme, a phoneme that has no differential character, nor any constant phonetic value, but whose function is to oppose the absence of a phoneme, before concluding:

We could similarly say, by schematising the conception that has been proposed here, that the function of mana-type notions is to oppose the absence of meaning without in itself having any particular meaning.[39]

Mana would be this floating signifier: a symbol in its pure state with zero symbolic value. It would be a semantic function guaranteeing the link between signifier and signified and opposing the absence of meaning without itself carrying any particular meaning.

It is this floating signifier that Lacan will take up, according to Zafiropoulos, under the heading of the Nom-du-père, ensuring the padding between signifiers and signifieds. Lacan takes it from his society, particularly from the symptoms of the obsessives who constitute its church. The Name-of-the-Father is to be situated alongside mana and orenda. It is this floating signifier, a zero symbolic value, whose function is to oppose the absence of signification without itself having any particular signification.

We cannot understand the emergence of a theory of the Name-of-the-Father in Lacan without understanding that it emerges in his return to

Freud in the 1950s, that is to say, in his return to the desire of the dead father of psychoanalysis, and under the effect of a new transference, to Freud first of all, but also to Lévi-Strauss [...] In our opinion, [...] we must re-grasp this Name-of-the-Father not at the level of content, but at the level of concept, as being a Lacanian reformulation of the semantic function of the signifier with a zero symbolic value which guarantees "that symbolic thought can be exercised", to speak as Levi-Strauss does.[40]

The absence of this function, without which the knotting between signifier and signified could not take place, characterised psychosis in 1956, while at the same time as Lévi-Strauss returned to what he called "institutional forms of the zero type", a category in which the function of the Name-of the-Father could be placed:

These institutions would have no intrinsic property, except to introduce the preconditions for the existence of the social system to which they belong, to which their presence—in itself devoid of meaning—allows it to be posited as a totality. Sociology thus encounters an essential problem, which it shares with linguistics, but of which it does not seem to have become aware in its own field. This problem consists in the existence of institutions devoid of meaning, if not to give meaning to the society that possesses them.[41]

The advance produced by Lacan's elaboration of the function of the Name-of-the-Father continues in its consequences at the level of the formation of the symptom in the following year's seminar devoted to phobia.[42] In Hans' case, it is indeed because the father does not respond that the phobia arises. The main feature of the phobia is therefore constituted by the appeal to a singular symbolic element that assumes a truly crystallising character. The object of the phobia is the horse. It is a signifier that compensates for the failure of the zero symbolic value of the Name-of-the-Father or "symbolic father" and metaphorises the mother's voracity. For Lacan, this signifier is a mythical formation. Here he takes up the notion of individual myth introduced in *Le mythe individuel du névrosé*.

... at the moment when it is called to the rescue to maintain the essential solidarity threatened by the gap introduced by the appearance of the phallus between the mother and the child, the element that intervenes in the phobia has a truly mythical character.[43]

It is a pure symbol. But what is a symbol in its pure state? It is a signifier-symbol, "recrystallizing" and solving the problem in its own way, but at the cost of the symptom, in this case the phobia. The symptom is first of all a symbol in its pure state, i.e.*not chained*, but unchained. Its deciphering and the resulting chaining will be responsible for making it a signifier. We will return later to the conditions necessary for its chaining. The symptom as mythical formation makes up for the hole left by the vacancy of the Name-of-the-Father. Later on, Lacan made the symptom an equivalent of the Name-of-the-Father or rather of its function, that of knotting the three registers: Symbolic, Imaginary and Real.

In the social system, symbolic thought produces a social, totemic and not individual symptom, God for example, responding to man's link to the law. But where Freud sees universals (Totem and Taboo, Oedipus), Lacan sees mythological modalities, historically and geographically differentiated. The operator of the regulation of "jouissance" is, indeed, the set of social rules formulated in the name of the dead father. It is in the name of the dead father that these rules would have introduced humanity to the register of the law and the prohibition of a part of jouissance whose Oedipal name is the Mother. For Freud, the signifier of exception would be the dead father, for Lévi-Strauss, it would be the signifier of zero value and for Lacan, the Name-of-the-Father. But in Lacan himself, the Name-of-the-Father as a signifier of exception will give way, later on, to another concept: the signifier of lacking in the Other, S (Ⱥ). The signifier of the incompleteness of the Other is a signifier that "can only be a trait that traces itself from its circle without being able to be counted in it".[44] Zafiropoulos concludes his study in the following terms:

> As soon as we identify the way in which the *Name-of-the-Father* partici-pates in a stabilisation of the subjective identity *via* the unary trait function—for instance, in the mirror experience—we can write that the subject is a function of the Other of the unary trait or again, and put differently, the son of the dead father. This stabilisation is clinically verified by the fact—as we have seen—that, in the case of degradation of the padding by the *Name-of-the-Father*, we observe in psychosis, the elabora-tion of a substitution (the delusion), and in phobia, a substitution of mythical appearance (the horse of little Hans for example). Myth and delusion emerge when the function of the unary trait is defective, as is the unity of the body itself by then.[45]

Lacan, referring to Ernest Jones's article on the symbol[46], will return to the function and place of symbols in 1959. Symbols, although "psycho-analytically repressed in the unconscious", do not themselves carry any indication of regression. It is therefore sufficient for them to make themselves heard in order to develop their effects. Hence, in our view, their function in analysis is that of developing the said effects through their appropriate evocation as a result of the analyst's intervention. The effectiveness of the interpretation will thus consist of *the capacity to evoke symbols underlying it.* If a so-called "signifier effect" is introduced, it is due to the mobilisation of symbols, thanks to the resources of language, and what constitutes them as symbols, in other words to the symbolic function at work.

Nevertheless, if Lévi-Strauss' structural anthropology is part of the foundation on which psychoanalysis, or at least Lacanian psychoanalysis, was built, it cannot account for some of its constructions. For Lévi-Strauss, the unconscious is an empty entity. It is an organ used to fabricate the symbolic, and the very idea of a conquest of unconscious knowledge no longer holds, as Annie Tardits points out, insisting on the ambiguity of the term "symbol" itself.

> The cohabitation under the same term of symbol of the symbolism at work in ritual and dreams on the one hand, and the mathematical writing used in scientific thought on the other, is not without question. The knot that makes up the structure of the symbol must be conceived under these two species.[47]

As we will see, Cassirer's works deal with that issue.

Duality of the symbol

The term symbol is used to designate that which represents something else, by virtue of an analogical correspondence. But it refers both to the elements of a rigorous algorithm, such as numerical signs, and to any concrete sign that evokes something absent or impossible to perceive by a natural relationship, for example the sceptre as a symbol of royalty.

On the one hand, there is a system of abstract signs which are signs of second intention and which presuppose the use of discourse before them. If there is an analogy, it is between the whole of the symbolic system and the whole of the system it is supposed to cover. It is a system governed by conceptual thought without empirical intuition, residing in the coherence of relationships. On the other hand, there are concrete signs, not organised in a system but maintaining a direct and natural term-to-term correspondence with what they symbolise.

The symbol is generally considered to be intermediate intermediary between the image and the sign. The sign implies a relation, however, in the image the relation is hidden. Symbolism essentially appears as the conquest of mediating relations, where each term is a purely differential, oppositional, relative and of negative value. For Ortigues, when we get closer to the material imagination, the differential function decreases and we tend towards equivalences; when we get closer to the formative elements of society, the differential function increases and we tend towards distinctive values[48]. But it is similarity that allows the identification of a trait that can then, or at the same time, be inserted into a system of differential values. This trait must be identified and counted as one. The symbol holds and retains the trait. A trait of the object is retained and the symbol is called upon so as to present this same trait even if it has other very different ones. *Only one trait is retained.*

How does the relationship between these two meanings of the symbol work and how does the subject move from one to the other? The term sign brings together the two categories of symbols. For Arrivé,[49] the opposition sign/symbol is not fixed in a constant way within the same linguistic system. There are also considerable variations from one lexical system to another. For example, Pierce's symbol has similar features to the Saussurean sign. Overall, it can be said that the term sign is favoured in works on semiotics and linguistics, although the terms "symbolic" and "symbolise" are also present in the discourse of linguists, while the term symbol is favoured in works that refer to psychoanalysis.

However, the term sign is also found in analytical literature, particularly in Lacan's work. Lacan uses the term sign in various places in his work, but with slightly different meanings:

- That of signifier, or sign/signifier[50] in reference to Freud's term *Zeichen* (Letter 52 to Fliess).
- The one that distinguishes it from the signifying order while at the same time attaching it to this order, in the seminar *Encore.*[51]

I want to finish by showing how the sign differs from the signifier. The signifier, I said, is characterised by representing a subject for another signifier. So, what is the sign about? Since time immemorial, the theory of knowledge, the conception of the world, has used the famous example of the smoke that does not exist without fire [...] Everyone knows that if you see smoke when you approach a desert island, you immediately think there is every chance that there is someone there who knows how to make fire. Until further notice, it will be another man. The sign is not, therefore, the sign of something, but of an effect which is what presupposes a signifying operation.

- That of the unary trait, which is clarified in the seminar *Transference*[52]. The sign is identified with the unary trait in this same lesson of the seminar on transference that we quoted in the previous chapter. It is the gaze of the Other that the subject internalises as a sign that constitutes the unique or unary trait that the subject will subsequently dispose of later, if he can, which is another question, in his relation to the signifier.

This is not to say that this *einziger Zug*, this unique trait, is given as a signifier. Not at all. It is quite probable, if we start from the dialectic that I am trying to sketch out before you, that it is possibly a sign. To say that it is a signifier, we would need more. It would have to be subsequently used in, or related to, a signifying battery. But what is defined by this *einziger Zug* is the punctuality of the original reference to the Other in the narcissistic relation.

A direction emerges which orients the relationship of these three terms: symbol, sign and signifier. The symbol is linked to the image, as in dreams. Nevertheless, it includes the trait, which is the vector of the analogy between the symbol and what it refers to. The symbol conveys one or more traits that the analysis of the dream must identify and then deploy. For the term sign, we prefer that of trait, or unary trait, which is of Lacan's third meaning. This seems to us to be much more fruitful since it is included in the definition of the symbol that we have just given, but also the start of the third term of the trio: the signifier. The signifier is derived from the unary trait on the condition that it can be used, that *is to say, that it can be connected: that it can find its place in a network*.

Dreams deploy the articulations of these three terms. In neurosis, the symbol summons the trait, the mark of the subject, which needs to be released or extracted from the symptom. The trait has been identified but repressed. The identificatory traits have been produced but covered by the superimpositions operated by the condensation from which they must be extracted. Conversely, psychosis establishes a short-circuit of the trait. Everything takes place as if we were passing directly from the trace to the word, or from the trace to the representation of words, to put it in Freudian terms, without the articulation of the representation of things. It is this articulation that the dream restores. The serial development of dreams completes the process. The trait attains the status of signifier through its insertion in dream series. It takes its place in a network that is woven around it as the dream sequences develop.

Notes

1 M. Mauss, *Sociologie et anthropologie* (Sociology and Anthropology) Paris, PUF, 1950.
2 B. Karsenti, *L'homme total, op. cit.*
3 Cl. Lévi-Strauss, preface à *Sociologie et anthropologie, op. cit.*
4 *Ibid, translated by us.*
5 *Ibid.*
6 Cl.Lévi-Strauss, *Anthropologie structurale*, Paris, Plon, 1974.
    Structural Anthropology, New York, Basic Books, 1963.
7 Cl.Lévi-Strauss, *La potière jalouse*, Paris, Plon, 2009.
    The Jealous Potter, University of Chicago Press, 1988).
8 Underlined by us.
9 *Ibid., translated by us.*
10 *Ibid.*
11 In *La potière jalouse*, Lévi-Strauss takes the step of a rather rapid and conventional criticism of Jung, even though the latter's thought is similar to his own on a lot of points.
12 *Ibid.*
13 *Freud-Jung Letters, op. cit.*
14 *La potière jalouse, op. cit.*
15 D. Boukhabza, *La lettre du rêve, un lecteur pour la psychose, op. cit.*
16 S. Freud, *The Unconscious* (1915), SE, Vol. XIV.
17 *La potière jalouse, op. cit.*
18 *Anthropologie structurale, op. cit.*
19 *Ibid.*
20 Underlined by us

21 *Ibid.*
22 M. Zafiropoulos, *Lacan et Lévi-Strauss ou le retour à Freud, 1951*–1957 (Lacan and Lévi-Strauss and the Return to Freud), Paris, puf, 2003.
23 J. Lacan, *Les complexes familiaux* (Family complexes), Autres Ecrits, Paris, Seuil, 2001.
   Three structural stages are differentiated: the weaning complex, the intrusion complex and the Oedipus complex. The intrusion complex, in particular, exposes the child to a major risk of narcissistic capture from which the Oedipus complex would, in principle, allow an escape.
24 *Lacan et Lévi-Strauss, op. cit.*
25 J. Lacan, *Introduction théorique aux fonctions de la psychanalyse en criminologie* (An Introduction to the Function of Psychonalysis in Criminology), Écrits, Paris, Seuil, 1966.
   Ecrits, The First Complete Edition in English, W.W. Norton & Co, 2006.
26 J. Lacan, *Le mythe individuel du névrosé, poésie et vérité dans la névrose* (The Individual Myth of Neurosis, Poetry and Truth in Neurosis), Paris, Seuil, 2007.
27 J. Lacan, *Fonction et champ de la parole et du langage* (Function and Field of Speech and Language), Écrits, *op. cit.*
28 *Ibid.* Translated by us
29 J. Lacan, *Le symbole et sa fonction religieuse (On Symbols and Their Religious Function)*, Le mythe individuel du névrosé, *op. cit.* Translated by us.
30 Underlined by us.
31 *Ibid.*
32 J. Lacan, *Le seminaire,* Livre I, Les écrits tecniques de Freud (Freud's Technical Writings), Seuil, 1975.
33 *Lacan et Levi-Strauss, op. cit.*
34 S. Freud, *The Interpretation of Dreams* (1900), SE Vol.IV-V.
35 J. Lacan, *Le séminaire,* Livre VIII, Le transfert (The Transference), Paris, Seuil, 1991.
36 *Ibid*, p.413. This single feature (*einziger Zug*) is then a sign and not yet a signifier. It would become one if it networked with others.
37 *Lacan et Lévi-Strauss, op. cit.*
38 Cl. Lévi-Strauss, *Préface à Sociologie et anthropologie, op. cit.*
39 *Ibid.*
40 M. Zafiropoulos, *Le transfert de Lacan à Lévi-Strauss*, L'anthropologie de Lévi-Strauss et la psychanalyse (The Transference of Lacan on Lévi-Strauss, Lévi-Strauss's Anthropology and Psychoanalysis), Éditions La Découverte, Paris, 2008.
41 Cl. Lévi-Strauss, *Anthropologie structurale, op cit.*
42 J. Lacan, *Le séminaire,* La relation d'objet (The Object Relation) Paris, Seuil, 1994.
43 *Ibid.* Translated by us.
44 J. Lacan, *Subversion du sujet et dialectique du désir dans l'inconscient freudien* (The Subversion of the Subject and the Dialectic of Desire in the Freudian Unconscious), Écrits, *op. cit.*
   The incompleteness of the symbolic order is a key point of Lacanian thinking and traces the border with Jung's thinking, for instance.
45 *Lacan et Levi-Strauss, op.cit.*
46 J. Lacan, *À Ernest Jones: Sur sa théorie du symbolisme* (On Ernest Jones' theory of symbolism), Écrits, *op. cit.*
47 A. Tardits, *Le ternaire et la pénombre du symbole* (The ternary and the shadows of symbols) Le transfert de Lacan à Lévi-Strauss, *op. cit.*

48 E Ortigues, *Le discours et le symbole* (Speech and Symbols) Paris, Beauchesne, 2007.
49 M. Arrivé, Le concept de symbole en sémio-linguistique et psychanalyse, Approche lexicologique du problème, *Documents de recherche,* CNRS, 1981.
50 J. Lacan, D'une question préliminaire à tout traitement possible de la psychose, *On a Question Prior to Any Possible Treatment of Psychosis,* Écrits, *op. cit.*
51 J. Lacan, *Le séminaire,* Livre XX, Encore, Paris, Seuil, 1975.
52 J. Lacan, Le transfert, *op. cit.*

Bibliography

Arrivé, M., Le concept de symbole en sémio- linguistique et psychanalyse, Approche lexicologique du problème, *Documents de recherche,* CNRS, 1981.
Ecrits, The first complete edition in English, W.W. Norton & Co, 2006.
Freud, S., *The unconscious,* Vol. XIV, SE, 1915.
Karsenti, B., *L'homme total, Sociologie, anthropologie et philosophie chez Marcel Mauss,* puf, Paris, 2007.
Lacan, J., *Introduction théorique aux fonctions de la psychanalyse en criminologie* (1950), Écrits, Paris, Seuil, 1966.
Lacan, J., *Fonction et champ de la parole et du langage* (1953), Ecrits, Paris, Seuil, 1966.
Lacan, J., *D'une question préliminaire à tout traitement possible de la psychose* (1958), Écrits, Paris, Seuil, 1966.
Lacan, J., *Subversion du sujet et dialectique du désir dans l'inconscient freudien* (1960), Écrits, Paris, Seuil, 1966.
Lacan, J., *À la mémoire d'Ernest Jones: Sur sa théorie du symbolisme* (1960) Écrits, Paris, Seuil, 1966.
Lacan, J., *Le séminaire,* Livre XX, Encore, Paris, Seuil, 1975.
Lacan, J., *Le séminaire,* Livre I, Les écrits techniques de Freud, Seuil, 1975.
Lacan, J., *Le séminaire,* Livre VIII, Le transfert, Paris, Seuil, 1991.
Lacan, J., *Le séminaire,* Livre III, La relation d'objet, Paris, Seuil, 1994.
Lacan, J., *Les complexes familiaux,* Autres Ecrits, Paris, Seuil, 2001.
Lévi-Strauss, Cl, préface à *Sociologie et anthropologie* de M.Mauss, PUF, Paris, 1950.
Lévi-Strauss, Cl, *Anthropologie structurale,* Plon, Paris, 1974.
Lévi-Strauss, Cl, *Structural Anthropology,* Basic Books, New York, 1963.
Lévi-Strauss, Cl, *La potière jalouse,* Plon, Paris, 2009.
The Jealous Potter, University of Chicago Press, 1988.
Mauss, M., *Sociologie et anthropologie,* PUF, Paris, 1950.
Ortigues, E., *Le discours et le symbole,* Beauchesne, Paris, 2007.
Tardits, A., *Le ternaire et la pénombre du symbole,* Le transfert de Lacan à.Lévi-Strauss, L'anthropologie de Lévi-Strauss et la psychanalyse, Éditions La Découverte, Paris, 2008.
Zafiropoulos, M., *Lacan et Lévi-Strauss ou le retour à Freud, 1951–1957,* (Lacan and Lévi-Strauss and the return to Freud), puf, Paris, 2003.
Zafiropoulos, M., *Le transfert de Lacan à Lévi-Strauss,* L'anthropologie de Lévi-Strauss et la psychanalyse Paris, Éditions La Découverte, 2008.

Chapter 3

Symbolic forms

Ernst Cassirer's thinking and his philosophy of symbolic forms allows a better understanding of the relations between the different aspects of symbols. Cassirer's works also enable us to clarify the ties between mythical thought and the unconscious.

Cassirer's work might not have been disseminated as widely as it deserved because of the circumstances of the historical period of his life. Born in 1876, one year after Jung, Cassirer was a German Jew. He was brought up in Berlin and became a professor of philosophy in Hamburg. He was close to Aby Warburg, the art historian and founder of the Warburg Library, who suffered from serious mental disorders and was hospitalised for a long time in Binswanger's clinic in Kreutzlingen. In 1933, Cassirer was forced to immigrate, first to England, then to Sweden and finally, in the early 1940s, to the United States, alongside Roman Jakobson. He collaborated with Jakobson and the journal *Word*, in which Lévi-Strauss also participated at that time. Despite a partly common field of investigation and their belonging to the same circle, Lévi-Strauss seems never to have mentioned Cassirer's works. Similarly, despite a common time, language and culture, and despite his connection to Warburg, it seems that Ernst Cassirer's path did not cross with psychoanalysis, which was then in full swing. Freud is barely mentioned in the *Philosophy of Symbolic Forms*. Only once is he mentioned in connection with *Totem and Taboo* and once in connection with agnosia. There is no mention of Jung, with whom he shares many sources: Schelling and theogony, Goethe and the creative imagination, Rudolph Otto and the sacred, Wundt and the method of associations, Lévy-Bruhl and primitive thought as well as an interest in myth and religion. Nevertheless, Cassirer's thinking appears to concern psychoanalysis very closely in that it is interested in symbolic "forms", in the relationships between these forms, but above all, and although this word is not used much by him, in symbolisation as a process. As a result, it meets, in many essential points, with our work on dreams as symbolic forms, or as pivots or mediators between symbolic forms.

The three volumes of Ernst Cassirer's *Philosophy of Symbolic Forms* were written between 1923 and 1929. Volume I is devoted to language, Volume II

DOI: 10.4324/b23380-4

to mythical thought and Volume III to the phenomenology of knowledge, with language having a special place as a vehicle for the transition from one form to another. For Cassirer, symbolic activities emerge from a common semiotic trunk, which is differentiated into different forms, or *directions of meaning*, which are not reduced to those previously mentioned and studied more precisely in his works. The various symbolic forms are anticipatory, and not explicitly present. They are collectively inherited and can coexist at the same time, the mythical form proving to be persistent.[1]

> The more richly and energetically the human spirit engages in its formative activity, the farther this very activity seems to remove it from the primal source of its own being. More and more, it appears to be imprisoned in its own creations—in the words of language, in the images of myth or art, in the intellectual symbols of cognition, which cover it like a delicate and transparent, but unbreachable veil. But the true, the profoundest task of a *philosophy* of culture, a philosophy of language, cognition, myth, etc., seems precisely to consist in raising this veil—in penetrating from the mediate sphere of mere meaning and characterization to the original sphere of intuitive vision. But, on the other hand the specific *organ* of philosophy—and it has no other at its disposal—rebels against this task. To philosophy, which finds its fulfilment only in the sharpness of the concept and in the clarity of "discursive" thought, the paradise of mysticism, the paradise of pure immediacy, is closed. Hence it has no other solution than to reverse the *direction* of inquiry, instead of taking the road back, it must attempt to continue forward. If a culture is manifested in the creation of specific image-worlds, of specific symbolic forms, the aim of philosophy is not to go behind these creations, but rather to understand and elucidate their basic formative principle.[2]

Furthermore, Cassirer establishes a link between the concept of serial-isation, specific to Goethean morphology, and the notion of structure developed by Jakobson. In addition to his poetic work, Goethe developed a scientific thought, oriented towards the natural sciences. For him, the diversity of plants can be reduced to the unity of a typical organ from which they are all derived through successive metamorphoses. Like Goethe, Cassirer did not want to separate the poetic part of Goethe's works from the botanical part. For Cassirer, Goethe's creation takes three basic forms: his life, his lyric poetry and his study of nature. For Cassirer, these are not three different aspects but three modes or forms of symbolisation. They are "three varieties of symbols, of one and the same relationship living in him". It is a question of working on the basis of structural homologies between life and works on the one hand, and between the works themselves on the other. Elements that seemed to be separate are arranged in series, according to a stable configuration, a connection and subordination governed by fixed principles. The internal forms are principles for the serialisation of Goethe's works and life; Cassirer seeks their law of development. Thus, a structural anthropology before the letter[3] takes shape. This does not exclude periods of opposition, parts of the same dynamic unity, with each creation being in some way a recreation of the previous one. A principle of development is the metamorphosis of one form into another and the associated renewal of the concept of form. The poet's creative imagination is governed by series of effective and fruitful points of reality as principles of a group of trans-formations.

> In it, we sum up an ever richer set of relations by which empirical elements, previously separated, are ordered into series, which manifest in themselves a stable configuration of their elements as well as a reciprocal connection and subordination according to fixed principles.[4]

As previously mentioned, both Cassirer and Lévi-Strauss participated in *Word*, the journal of the New York Linguistic Circle, alongside Roman Jakobson. However, there is a notable gap between Lévi-Strauss' and Cassirer's thinking. For Cassirer, there is a primacy of ritual over myth, unlike for Lévi-Strauss. For Cassirer, at the beginning is the action; the gestures are already manifestations of the symbolic function. The space of the myth is constructed from the acting human body. The ritual is essentially an affective ritual, with the expression of affects being already the work of the symbolic function.

Mythical thinking

For Cassirer, the specific productions of the mind cannot be understood without relating them to their foundation: the universality and the lack of differentiation of mythic consciousness, considered as a modality of thought in its own right, and to the way in which these productions of mind have been able to detach themselves from it.[5] The development of science can only be grasped on the condition that it is shown how it proceeds from mythical immediacy and develops from it, according to principles. Cassirer, referring to Schelling, supports a non-allegorical interpretation of myth, an interpretation according to which meaning emerges from its very development. For Schelling, the mythological process is a theogonic process in which God becomes himself, and through which he gradually manifests himself as the true God. This development is determined by the passage from the unity of God, mere existence without self-consciousness, to plurality and from this plurality to its opposite, the true and recognised unity of God. Human consciousness in the proper sense is not external to God and contains within itself the relation to God, not by an effect of knowledge but by the force of its very nature. Consciousness must pass through the crisis of polytheism, that of split and particularisation before returning to monotheism and the emergence of an absolute God.[6] Conversely, the anthropogonic perspective takes as its starting point the empirical unity of human nature considered as the original and constitutive factor of the mythical process, which would explain why it develops in an identical way, in multiple temporal and spatial points. Humanity is only constituted by the totality of its activities, Cassirer insists a lot on this point, at the beginning is the action or rather the activity, and it is through this set of activities that the divorce between subject and object progressively takes place.

For the Kantian critical philosophy to which Cassirer refers, objects are not given to consciousness and the relation of the representation to the object presupposes a spontaneous and autonomous act of the latter. The image of the world is only possible through a particular act of objectification that "informs" simple impressions into representations. The spatial setting up of the world of perception involves acts of identification, differentiation, comparison and attribution. The being of objects depends on a relation of time and measure and is constituted from them:

> Over and over again the constant is differentiated from the variable, the objective from the subjective, truth from appearance: and it is through this movement that the certainty, the true logical character of empirical thinking, is gained. The positive reality of the empirical object is constituted through a double negation: through its differentiation from the "absolute" on the one hand and from sensory appearance on the other. This object appears "phenomenal" but it is not "illusory," since it is grounded in necessary laws of knowledge, since it is a *phaenomenon bene fundatum*. Thus we see that in the sphere of theoretical thought the general concept of objectivity as well as its concrete realizations rest on a progressive *analysis* of the elements of experience, on a critical operation of the intellect in which the "accidental" is progressively differentiated from the "essential," the variable from the constant.[7]

The characteristics of mythical thought and its modalities of operation are therefore to be specified in order to identify the way that the critical work of the mind would then confront them. Many of these characteristics are found in dreams as well as in delusion.

Lack of differentiation and mythic construction

Mythical thinking does not recognise the discriminations made by logical thinking, hence the lack of differentiation that reigns in it, and is nevertheless relative since it also proceeds to groupings, but according to its own criteria which are not those of logical thinking.

Thing and meaning

The mythical world is not concrete because it deals only with objective contents and excludes all abstract contents, i.e. everything that is sign and meaning. It is concrete in that the thing and its meaning merge and are developed together into an immediate, concretised unity. Figures that arise in myths are something objective, but the relation to these figures does not yet manifest anything of that decisive crisis, Cassirer says, that generates empirical and conceptual knowledge. The reality that it grasps is homogeneous and undifferentiated; dream and wakefulness and life and death merge. The division of the real and the ideal and the opposition between the image and the thing are foreign to him. Where we see an allegorical representation, myth sees a relationship *of real identity*. The image does not manifest the thing, it is the thing. The powerlessness of mythic thought to grasp signifying activity is manifest in the relationship between myth and language, which condition each other. The word and the name do not signify: they "are" and "act", especially the proper name which maintains a relationship of identity with the one it designates and even more so the name of the god which constitutes a real part of its essence and its effectiveness. The Old Testament demonstrates this in an exemplary way with the power of God's name reaching its climax.

Time and space

The mythical sense of space unfolds from the opposition of day and night. All the separations and articulations produced between the domains of mythical space are determined by this difference. Only when a content is spatially determined, when it is delimited and distinguished from the indistinct totality of space, does it acquire an autonomous existence. The act of separating makes it *ex-sistere*—exist. The opposition of day and night, together with the opposition of the holy and the profane, orientates the division of space into quarters and constitutes the spatial oppositions that particularise mythical space with its cardinal gods—gods of the east and north, of the west and south, gods of the lower world and of the higher world. Places and directions are separated because they are assigned a meaning and receive opposite values within the mythical world.[8]

But myth as such, *muthos*, implies a much temporal perspective than a spatial one. Instead of distinguishing relative degrees of temporality, mythic consciousness remains in a state of lack of differentiation and indivisible time. The division of space into regions and directions is parallel to the division of time into singular moments. These moments do not constitute a series but are given a form—a qualitative nature. However, time, unlike space, manifests a univocal and irreversible meaning, that is the meaning of its flow. The passage from a feeling of temporality to the concept of time comprises three different stages that language will name. At the beginning, only the present and the non-present are opposed. Then, in relation to the construction of the notion of causality, comes the notion of succession and from there the notion of a temporal order that will unify the event. Then, in relation to action, other differentiations arise, such as the durable and the momentary. But above all, because of the intuition of the temporal unity of the action, which starts from the subject whose concept is already involved in the action, as well as the goal of the action itself, the action can no longer be fragmented into singular phases. Behind it, the unifying energy of the subject and the equally unifying aim and end of the action manifest themselves. This is how the moments of the action come together to form a global series and give rise to the unity of the representation of time.

Similarity and identity

The category of similarity also opposes myth and knowledge. If in order to organise the chaos of perceptible impressions, mythical thought, like scientific thought, draws out series of similarities, the capture of these similarities is carried out in different ways. The category of similarity does not apply because of the agreement between perceptible clues and conceptual milestones but is conditioned by the law of magical coherence. Everything corresponding to and favouring each other in magic comes together in the unity of a mythical genre. It is sufficient for mythical thought to discover a similarity in a perceptible phenomenon in order to gather the forms in which this similarity appears into a single mythical genre, as witness to an identity of essence.

Simultaneity and causality

The nature of mythical thinking can be further grasped by analysing the concept of causality. In mythical thinking, every contemporaneity, every contact and every coexistence imply a causal consequence. But above all, mythical thinking does not allow any division in a representation in order to isolate its elements. Therefore, where logical thinking, which is the basis of the principle of causality, begins by positing and *identifying* elements, mythical thinking does not produce any such discrimination. This is why, where empirical thinking about causality speaks of change, mythical thinking knows only metamorphosis. But, even more so, where in the empirical conception the whole is composed of parts, mythical thought does not perceive differences. The whole has no parts, and the part is, and functions as, the whole. This form of thinking, which is found in the field of time as well as of space, pervades the grasp of the successive and the simultaneous, which are neglected and replaced by causal relations.

Pars pro toto

Mythical and linguistic thinking are closely intertwined and proceed from a common root: that of metaphorical thinking. Schelling saw in language "a bloodless mythology" which retains, in arbitrary and formal distinctions, what mythology contains in the form of living and concrete distinctions. Cassirer stood outside the debate on the priority of language or myth in the constitution of metaphor and distinguished a "radical" metaphor as a condition for the formation of language and, at the same time, as a condition for the formation of mythical concepts. The most primitive linguistic externalisation already involved the transposition of a content of intuition or feeling into sound, a radically heterogeneous medium, just as a certain impression is torn from the sphere of the habitual to take on a sacred character. The question does not arise of an antecedence of linguistic form or mythical form, but rather there is an indissoluble correlation between language and myth, from which both only gradually emerge. They are the different branches of a single impulse of symbolic shaping. Like the production of the "gods of the moment", any intensification of sensitive intuition is the root of any formatting, linguistic or mythical. But, if in the case of logical thought, concentric extension over wider domains and concepts is the rule, linguistic and mythical concepts are constituted in an opposite movement. Intuition is concentrated on a single point on which the emphasis of meaning will be placed. Everything outside it remains invisible and insignificant. It is the principle of *pars pro toto* that characterises magical thinking and its rituals, but also its practices, based on the magic of analogy. In the case of myth, it is not a question of substituting a rhetorical figure but of *a true and immediate identity*. This process is at work in the constitution of both language and myth, in mutual interaction. But language does not only belong to the domain of myth, another force acts in it which will make the word of language the sign of the concept.

For our empirical apprehension the whole consists of its parts; for the logic of natural science, for the logic of the analytical scientific concept of causality, it results from them; for the mythical view neither of these propositions applies; here there prevails a true indifference, both in thought and practice, between the whole and its parts. The whole does not "have" parts and does not break down into them; the part is immediately the whole and functions as such. This relationship, this principle of the pars pro toto has also been designated as a basic principle of primitive logic. However, the part does not merely represent the whole, but "really" specifies it; the relationship is not symbolic and intellectual, but real and material. The part, in mythical terms, is the same thing as the whole, because it is a real vehicle of efficacy—because everything which it incurs or does is incurred or done by the whole at the same time.[9]

Differentiation

Numeracy

The differentiation of numerical relations, like that of spatial relations, starts from the human body and its members, but the act of counting does not progress arbitrarily from one part of the body to another: the right hand follows the left, the breast follows the neck, the shoulders, the hands and the feet, according to a precise order chosen and maintained by convention. This ordering allows the mind to progress from the determination of things to that of acts and then, through the connections and divisions it makes, to the principle of number formation. However, for a long time, numeration remains attached to the qualities of the object and language sticks to the diversity of objects and their properties. Any number is not valid for any thing. The tendency of language is rather to subordinate the quantitative difference to the generic difference and to modify it according to the latter. Whereas number, in order to grasp coexistence in a collection, relies on the intuition of space, it needs the intuition of time to specify the notion of distributive unity and individuality. It is in space that the moment of juxtaposition and inclusion of elements appears, whereas it is in time that their succession and reciprocal exclusion are apprehended, thus their belonging to a series. The thought of number takes these two aspects at its service in order to express plurality through language, as a collection on the one hand, and as singularisation and particularisation on the other. However, the formation of number also comes from another source on the side of subjectivity. It would be less the juxtaposition and reciprocal exclusion of objects than *the demarcation of the "I" and the "You"* that would have allowed the consciousness of number to emerge. The opposition of the One and the Multiple is much more sensitive. The first numerical determinations invented by language come not from the differentiation of things but from those of persons. The opposition of the "I" and the "You" gives rise to the one and the two. A much more important step will lead to the three, the sequence of numbers being even more difficult to establish. Numeration is very closely linked to the intuition of the "I", the "You" and the "Him/Her" and is only realised very gradually. Hence the particular role assigned to the numbers one, two and three as creations of a particular kind. But as the idea of a numerical series constructed according to a unitary principle becomes established, each number, instead of representing a particular content, will become a simple position equivalent to the others.

Serialisation and conceptualisation

To study concepts is to study words and names. The validity of the concept can be reduced to the validity and fruitfulness of the word. Are the characteristics according to which we divide objects into classes given to us before the formation of language or is it language itself that provides them? What are the conditions of this primitive shaping which takes place in language and which forms the basis of all subsequent syntheses of logical thought? It is precisely at the moment of the creation of a language and its words that we discover the fundamental form of thought: objectification. It is a matter of freezing the content and designating it through the modification of impressions as a self-similar and recurring being. But the singular quality does not only possess a specific state, it is also related to others through this state.

When we gather contents after having fixed and named them in the form of a series, *we have posited a common being that specifies itself in the singular elements of the series.* It manifests itself in them all, but in each of them with a nuance, a difference of its own. Language takes a further step towards generic universality when, instead of merely inventing terms for certain areas of intuition, it comes to associate the terms themselves. The actual coappearance of contents can be clearly manifested in the linguistic form itself, for example when groups of different words are characterised as elements of the same set by a common prefix or suffix. When language makes this co-relationship of contents visible, it already serves as a vehicle for intellectual progress, even if it does not yet succeed in designating what constitutes this relationship. At the bottom of the scale is the classification by analogy, as long as there is a certain resemblance between the perceptible impressions provoked by the objects. Class distinctions, based on the determination of a relationship, belong to another stratum of thought. The human body and its members are also one of the first foundations of linguistic orientation. The form of the construction of the series is never determined by objective similarity alone, but also follows the course of the subjective imagination and the themes that direct language in the construction of classes are often related to the mythical forms themselves.

The concept is the general term of a series which designates the rule of succession of its individual terms. The sign is never a simple, accidental and external envelope of the idea, but a certain orientation, a tendency and a primary form of the thoughts which are expressed in its use. Language does not limit itself to designating impressions; the act of naming always implies, at the same time, *a change of form.* Scientific knowledge reproduces the same process. It reaches the proximity of nature only by learning to renounce it by pushing the given into an ideal distance. The sequence of perceptions, the serial form of empirical coexistence and succession, poses a question to be resolved with the resources of the serial form of concepts. But both keep their forms quite distinct. The renewed contact with empirical intuition brings the concept to its autonomous development but perception is only the intercessor. Between empirical and ideal elements, there is no possible relationship of similarity. An isolated "form" cannot be made to correspond to an isolated "thing"; the two arrangements can only relate to and measure each other in their totality. This work of differentiation performed by language starting from its mythical roots and never totally achieved would be the dream's major undertaking

Mythical consciousness

The construction of the world image begins with the separation between appearance and truth, perceived and represented, subjective and objective. The mythical consciousness lives in the perceptible impression without measuring it against anything else; for it, the impression is absolute. Mythical consciousness does not possess the object by constructing it but rather it is *possessed by it*. Myth can be conceived as an attempt to make the objective world of phenomena disappear into the subjective mode and interpret it according to the categories of the latter. It is only in and through symbolic forms that inside and outside, self and reality, are defined and bounded by each other. It is a boundary that is not drawn once and for all, and whose course is different for each of these forms. It is only very slowly that the mythical category of soul gives rise to the category of the self and to the idea of person and personality, essentially through action and its link to desire. But the self knows itself only on condition that it grasps itself as a member of a community, a clan, a tribe or a social group. The mythical and religious consciousness can be considered as one of the conditions of the social structure and feeling of community and at the principle of its organisation.

For empirical knowledge, objects are grouped into species and genera less because of their differences or similarities and more because of their causal dependence. For mythical intuition, the origin of generic unity is quite different; it is magical in nature. It confuses in a single figure the terms that it considers as correlative from a magical point of view, such as man and animal. The hunter or the shepherd immediately feels united with the animal in their activity, they feel dependent on it and in a close relationship. But this community also extends to very different regions of life, leading to a division of the universe according to "affinities" which divides it into mythically separate genera and species, but preserving with strength the idea of the unity of life; the primary feeling of community extends to the totality of the living. It is art alone which, in helping man to give an image of himself, discovers at the same time what the specific idea of man can be. The path of interiority can only be followed if it joins the seemingly opposite path from the inside to the outside in activities. All activities are formative in a double sense. The self is not only satisfied with imposing a form on objects but receives back from them, through feedback, what shapes it itself. This is particularly true of the relationship between man and the divine world.

The gods

The world of the gods is constructed with reference to human activity. Consciousness can only distinguish between the different fields of activity by relating them to a stable centre, such as a single mythical figure. It is only

through mediating elements, the gods of activity, that action can be apprehended. It is through its mythical exponents, the gods of activity, "special
gods", that consciousness comes to know itself and that man also comes to
perceive himself. Man apprehends his action only on the condition that he
distances himself from it and projects it outwards. From this projection, the
figure of the god, the civiliser, is born, as the first mythical emergence of the
cultural consciousness that begins to develop. Man's own self is only found
through the diversions of the divine self. The metamorphosis into "personal
gods" constitutes the next stage, with the corollary of *the advent of the proper
name*, establishing the stable core of mythical representation. It is through the
movement towards the general and the tendency towards abstraction that the
individualisation determining the personal gods takes place.

As the multiplicity of objects related to action grows, the energy of the action
as such, i.e. *the consciousness of the acting subject,* is more and more clearly
distinguished. The self is grasped as a concrete unity, identical to itself, which
gathers the various orientations of action. This mediating element, the god,
enables the self to free itself from the materiality of action. In the same way, the
multiplication of particular deities allows for refocusing on the origin of the
divine efficiency that is to conceive a creative principle. A new conception of
man, ethical and spiritual, corresponds to the mutation of the notion of god.
For man is not satisfied with transferring his own personality onto the god and
attributing to him the consciousness he has of himself; it is thanks to the figure
of the god that he can find his self-awareness.

Names of gods

Name and being have an inner and necessary relationship. The name does not
only designate the being, it is the being itself and the force of the being that is
contained in it; these are the fundamental presuppositions of the mythic
intuition. For Max Müller, one of Cassirer's references, myth is related to a
fundamental "lacking" in language, one of its original weaknesses, that of *its
equivocality.* Myth is nothing more than the dark shadow cast by thought on
language. In the myth of Daphne, she is pursued by Apollo and then saved by
her mother, the earth, who turns her into a laurel tree. The name Daphne,
laurel in Greek, can also be traced back to the Sanskrit Ahanâ which means
redness of the dawn. The content of the myth simply transcribes the etymology, i.e. the glow of the dawn and the rising of the solar god who rushes
behind Daphne then her disappearance into the bosom of mother earth as she
is transformed into a laurel tree. From this point on, the question of the
relationship between names and concepts arises, without any a priori antecedence of one or the other.

In his study of the relationship between language and myth,[10] Cassirer
draws on the work of Hermann Usener's *The Names of Gods: An Essay on the
Formation of Religious Concepts*. In examining the creation and formation of

the concepts of gods from their names, he distinguishes three successive phases:

- The earliest period of mythical thought is characterised by the formation of the so-called "gods of the moment". Any impression that reaches man is likely to assume a religious character. A concept or any object that dominates the thought in the moment can attain the rank of a deity.
- With the development of culture, another series of gods, which does not have its origin in momentary sensation but in a durable and ordered activity, appears, no longer related to suffering but to action. These are the "special gods", connected to a specific domain. Having cross-checked different cultural spheres, Usener considers that the figures and names of the "special gods" are present everywhere in a more or less similar way in a certain phase of religious development. As long as the name is understood in connection with its original meaning, it will endure.
- However, if through phonic mutation or root decay, the name loses its connection with its original domain, it will become a proper name, evoking the idea of a specific personality. This is how "personal gods" come about.

What interests Usener above all is what results from these observations as a law of formation governing the sphere of the religious. In contrast to logical thought, which groups and orders in ever larger ensembles according to distinctive features, mythical thought is a prisoner of its content; instead of enlarging or extending it concentrates without mediation, which is what Usener calls "god of the moment". The question then arises as to how something lasting could have become detached from this process. The "gods of the moment" will acquire an existence of their own when detached from the instant that saw their birth, as we have seen in the mythical apprehension of time. This is where language comes in, with the persistence and the fixation in the phoneme. Only symbolic expression creates the possibility of retrospective or predictive vision. What has been produced once does not disappear again once the phoneme has put its stamp on it. Subsequently, the different spheres of action invest language correlatively but also disinvest it with the corresponding linguistic mutations when certain interests have fallen into disuse. The rooting of linguistic consciousness in mythico-religious consciousness is expressed in the fact that linguistic figures first appear as mythic figures.[11] In creation stories, the word is related to the creator god, either as his instrument or as the foundation from which he himself proceeds; the name of the god embodies him. Discursive thinking moves towards enlargement, linking and systematisation. The mythical and linguistic vision, on the other hand, aims at concentration, condensation and enhancement through isolation. It removes and samples and it is only when the separation succeeds that the mythical or linguistic figure is born. The word must be grasped in its mythical sense as a being, before it can be grasped in its ideal sense as an organon of the mind.

The potential between "symbol" and "meaning" is resolved; in place of a more or less adequate "expression," we find a relation of identity, of complete congruence between "image" and "object," between the name and the thing.[12]

But the three phases highlighted by Usener must also be reviewed in the light of another concept that subsequently came to flesh out the history of religions, that is, the concept of mana. The category of mana can be considered emblematic of mythical and religious thought. Mana, a supernatural, indeterminate and eminently mobile and transferable force, imposes a sacred character to which the term taboo corresponds on a negative level. Universal in character, it can be found in the manitou of the Algonquins, the wakanda of the Sioux and the orenda of the Iroquois. It is also undifferentiated, this undifferentiation being in a way one of the marks of the concept; it is a property rather than a determined entity, an anonymous attribute of the mythico-religious order, inducing the separation of the world of the sacred from that of the profane. Mana denotes the original mythico-religious attribution. Cassirer joins Lévi-Strauss' concept but weaves a slightly different thread in connection with the attribution of a property and its progressive naming thanks to the identification and enhancement of the mythico-linguistic common trunk. The contents of mythical consciousness, individualised with the immediacy and intensity that are proper to it, come together to form a whole, characterised by the same colouring that sets it apart from the usual and the everyday. It confers on it a transcendent character, at once unveiling and concealing, the mark of the mythical and religious universe, its sacred character; it is here that Cassirer quotes Rudolph Otto.[13] This sacredness can imprint any content and does not indicate a constitution proper to the object but a mode of relation to this object. In fact, the concept of mana belongs to a level preceding even the gods of the moment in which it will later incarnate as well as in the subsequent phases:

At this point, mythic thinking veers from its original, "anonymous" stage to the exact opposite, the phase of "polynomy". Each deity unites in itself a wealth of attributes, which originally belonged to the special gods that have all been combined in a new god. Their successor, however, inherits not only all their attributes, but also their names—not as his proper name but as appellatives; for the name and nature of the god are the same thing. Thus the polynomy of the personal deities is an essential trait in their very being.[14]

Personal gods became endowed with what were initially the attributes and at the same time the names of special gods. For instance, Isis, the Egyptian goddess, appears as the thousand names or even ten thousand names goddess, and Allah's power is illustrated in the Koran with his hundred names.

Later still, the joint development of mythical thought and language will lead to the opposite phenomenon of seeking the unity of the concept of god, and consequently being unable to designate it by any name. The divine then becomes a being without properties because any property would limit its own essence. The divine excludes all particular attributes and can only draw its predicates from itself. The continuous construction of the mythical world is thus matched by its constant overcoming; a position and its negation belong equally to the mythical consciousness. Similarly, in the world of writing, the image is at first a substitute for the object that actually replaces it, and writing belongs at its birth to the world of magic, serving to take possession of the object or to protect it. The writing must therefore be identical to what it wants to represent. Writing must lose this affective colouring in order to move from the real to the ideal. Similarly, religious thought itself must move away from the mythical thought with which it is interwoven. The specific nature of the religious form manifests itself in the new attitude of consciousness towards the mythical image. The consciousness will then separate itself from the mythical image by introducing the opposition between meaning and existence. The reality of "things" is transformed in the religious conception into a world of signs that defines the specifically religious perspective. The perceptible and the spiritual no longer coincide but refer to each other in an analogical relationship that has the character of an allegory or even anagogy, moving from the visible to the invisible.

What interests us in Cassirer is not only the way in which he specifies the characteristics of mythical thought, but above all the demonstration that he produces of the links uniting mythical thought and language, their common roots, from which language will produce more and more differentiations. Of course, nowhere does Cassirer refer to psychoanalysis and he does not take into account, except on a few rare occasions, the way in which language is transmitted through the relationship with the other. As a counter-example, we can cite the development of numbers and its preferential connection to the human relationship as the very thing that temporarily hinders the creation of the number sequence. We will give an example of this in a case study in the last chapter. The relation to the other is not, therefore, the field in which Cassirer's thought is particularly exercised. Nevertheless, everything that is said about the constitution of the object, the separation of subject/object and the constitution of the "self" can be extrapolated from the human relationship if the other is placed in the place of the "object". The journey accomplished by mythical thought, supported by language, leads it to separate the subject from the object, from all types of objects, including the other.

The emergence of the feeling of self from the mythical feeling of the unity of life is accompanied by the advent of religion, whose development follows the progress of mythical consciousness. Language produces the necessary nominations—in the form of the "gods of the moment", "special gods" then "personal gods"—before the reunification that will produce monotheism, where the nomination procedure is reversed in order to bar the name of God, and at the same time withdraws all attributes. Religious thought is distinguished from the mythical thought with which it was intertwined. Consciousness separates itself from myth by measuring the gap between meaning and existence, or between the perceptible and the spiritual. The divine is thus first linked to the object, to activity, then personified with its attributes to be then reduced to the One, devoid of properties but also of name. The journey from the mythical to the religious goes hand in hand with that of consciousness, which grasps itself as one in the face of a less and less particularised God. This progression of the mythical consciousness that comes to grasp itself as one, in other words this advent of the subject, takes place by means of and through its relation to the religious. It is through its relationship to the divine and the successive nominations engendered by this relationship that subjectivity emerges.

The unconscious: a mythical thought

The characteristics of mythical thought, its lack of differentiation and its constructions are those of unconscious thought, those of Freud's primary process as it manifests itself vividly in dreams, but also as it constitutes the background of the productions of psychosis or it activates and determines the processes of the symptom formation. But, if their common denominator consists in their connection with mythical thought, dreams, delusion and symptom are not on the same level. Dreams need to be distinguished from delusion and symptom by their rule of formation. Symbols in dreams are closely submitted to a condition, that of the figuration of unconscious "thoughts". But are they really thoughts? Can we speak of thoughts in the face of such organisations as dreams where, as Freud insists, logical relations are lacking?[15] Is it not rather a defect in the production of thoughts that provokes the call for dreams? A defect fertilised by dreams which, precisely, provide the necessary materials for these "pre-thoughts" to emerge, to construct themselves and to knot themselves into articulated thoughts. This pre-thought, which it is not a misnomer to call mythical thought, produces the necessary differentiations in order to represent the impressions that triggered it with the help of this other symbolic formation, constantly connected to the first one in dreams, language. Dreams are a symbolic form, to use Cassirer's term, and a particular symbolic form in the sense that dreams, mythically constructed on their surface, in their manifest content, mythically undifferentiated, possess within themselves the organ of their deciphering. This organ is language, associated with mythical thought in their common trunk, their association being revealed by the figures of dreams as a work in progress. In dreams, language and mythical thought intertwine and their disentanglement is at the basis of their deciphering. The interpretation of the dream, if it happens, will pursue the deciphering-ciphering task, since these two movements are constantly associated, through the enunciation of the dream and the implementation of the discriminative work of language.

Concrescence and rebus

We have shown the difficulty of mythical thinking in grasping signifying activity and its manifestation in the relationship between myth and language. Mythical thought merges the thing and its meaning, i.e. the field of reality and that of ideas. The word and the name do not signify, they exist and act like things. Mythical thinking ignores the difference, even the opposition, between the image and the thing. The image does not manifest the thing, it is the thing.

The impressions that trigger dreams cannot be used as they are. They need to be transformed into a pictorial language, relying on the points of contact and identities that are the supports of dream work. Symbols are the first modality of representation. As we saw in the example of the plane indicating a "rough" passage of a presentation, an example borrowed from Silberer and taken up by Lévi-Strauss, it is not so much the passage from the abstract to the concrete that is important, but rather the linking of one to the other, that is to say, the passage from an unconscious thought, whose materials of choice are images and symbols, to a thought expressed in linguistic terms. Dreams achieve the link between these two registers through their use of images. The unconscious trace first appears in images which is the characteristic of dreams, then these images call for words. This is the function of the rebus. The interpretation of dreams as a rebus implies renouncing any totalising interpretation and instead replacing each image with a syllable or a word.

The rebus function of dreams can also be related to the differentiation between representations of words and representations of things indicated by Freud in his article *The Unconscious*.[16] The representation of object investment is split between word representation and thing representation. While the conscious representation consists of the thing representation plus the corresponding word representation, the unconscious representation consists of the thing representation alone. The thing representation is realised through the investment of the memory traces of things. It is precisely from the point of view of schizophrenia that the question is addressed. In schizophrenia, the libido withdraws into the ego and the object investments are abandoned to reach an "anobjectal" state, a state before the constitution of the object, comparable to primary narcissism. But words are also treated in a particular way. Words are subjected to the same process as in dreams (the primary process) and its agent (the displacement-condensation couple), and Freud cites the work of Bleuler and Jung in support of this idea. But, in the case of schizophrenia, it is the identity of verbal expressions and not the similarity of things that commands the substitution. The word relation predominates over the thing relation. What characterises schizophrenia, unlike the so-called transference neuroses, is this absence of overlapping between word and thing. The investment of the word representation, preserved in schizophrenia, is due to the fact that the word representation would not be concerned by repression. Its continued investment would rather correspond to an attempt at restitution, meaning an attempt to recover lost objects by this means. There is thus a rupture of the link between representations of words and representations of things; there is a delinking. It is this link that is damaged and it is this link that needs to be restored.

It is at this point that we situate the privileged role that dreams play, via regression, in this connection between representations of words and representations of things. If the representation of things is abandoned, it is the consequence of the disinvestment of the corresponding mnemonic traces due to the vagaries of the objectal relationship. The disinvestment of the mnemonic traces is an avatar of the objectal relation. If we hold the thread that runs through *On Narcissism: an introduction*, for the schizophrenic it is indeed following a frustration, the refusal of satisfaction of a pulsional claim, that the libido is detached from the objects to withdraw into the ego. The restoration of the object relation, which the transference carries out, is able to produce *de facto* the reinvestment of the mnemonic traces that dreams and their symbolism translate. The representations of things, pending, unrealised and fixed in the form of mnemonic traces (or signs of perception, these two terms are equivalent for us) are able then to arise and be linked to the representations of words, completing the process.

The dream enunciated in the transference process thus fulfils its purpose. It is the regression in dreams that allows the reinvestment of the traces in abeyance and the production of the representations of things, thanks to the figuration of dreams and their *call for figurability*. Regression reinvests the signs of perception, which are then transformed, and forced by the necessity of figuration to be realised in representations of things in the form of the images of the dream. The traces of perception are transformed into representations of things, supported by the images, and wait to be connected to the representations of words, resulting from the collective experience that works in language. It is the recourse to images that gives the dream its value as an exemplary tool for the production of this relationship and founds its effectiveness, in particular but not exclusively, in the treatment of psychoses. It is the connection between things and words that stops the slippage of meaning in schizophrenia and determines a stopping or padding point. This process necessarily transits through symbols and images, as connecting figures and *bridges* between things and words, conscious and unconscious.

This brings us back to the non-verbal character of the symbol. We can relate it to the necessity of representation in images—"writing in images"—themselves linked to the traces of perceptions, as a moment and an indispensable stage for the connection between words and things. But this representation would not be the vector of any progress if dreams carried by language were not also enunciated, if symbols did not take their place through enunciation, to characterise human exchange.

Pars pro toto: the symbol, vehicle of the trait

Let us return to the role of symbols and their palliative function on the defect of primordial identification, starting from the case of the seamstress presented by Jung in *Psychology of Dementia Praecox*. It is the prevalence of unconscious complexes and their impact on associations in dementia praecox that must be demonstrated. The test of associations is carried out on a 60-year-old patient, a former seamstress, who had been in the clinic for twenty years. The word Socrates, present in the delusion, is used as an inducing word. The test shows the identification of the patient with Socrates on the basis of at least two features: like Socrates, she is a wise man or a professor in her field and, like Socrates, she was slandered and then imprisoned. Nevertheless, as we indicated, she is unable to perceive these common features of Socrates' and her own background as vectors of her identification with him. Identification as identification with a trait cannot be perceived as such. She is not like Socrates, she is Socrates. A feature of Socrates is identical to the whole of Socrates, according to mythical thought and the *pars pro toto* metaphor, of which the delusional metaphor takes the form. Unlike the empirical conception where the whole is made up of parts, mythical thinking does not perceive differences. As in myth, the substitution is not based on a rhetorical figure but it is the product of *a true and immediate identity*. The part does not represent the whole, as in metonymy, it is identical to the whole. The identification with Socrates cannot be identified as such. Socrates, in the place of a symbol in the delusion, compensates for what could not happen in the patient, i.e. the inscription of a trait identifying the passage of the subject. The hyper-symbolism of schizophrenia appears to be a compensation for the lack of symbolisation, just like that of dreams, but, unlike dreams, without any possibility of elaboration.

Similarity and figuration of the trait

The thoughts of dreams come from several centres, however, these centres have points of contact.[17] A stream of thoughts directed in one direction often has another stream directed in the opposite direction. This can be explained by the fact that dreams never represent contradiction but are content to unite opposites with the help of different processes of figuration, or sometimes even to reverse a current into its opposite. Only one logical relationship is preserved and put forward in the formation of dreams, that of the resemblance; we find again the notion of a point of contact. This resemblance is translated by the dream work with the help of specific processes. At the forefront of these processes is condensation. The resemblance is represented by the fusion into a unit that is already present in dream material (identification) or that is formed on this occasion (composite formation).[18] In the first case, a trait or a feature, for it is the figuration of the trait that is at issue, is represented, carried by one person and sometimes recurrently in a set of dreams. In the second case, one person carries several traits belonging to several other persons involved in the dream material. This process of bringing together several occurrences of the same trait to form a new, wholly imaginary unit is one of the principles underlying mythic thinking, as we have seen. It is sufficient for mythic thought to discover a similarity in order to bring together the forms in which this similarity is found into a single mythic genre, as witness to an identity of essence. The elements that are corresponding to each other, are brought together under the heading of a new genre.

This "mythical" way of proceeding, however, has the result of identifying a trait, or an attribute, through its different occurrences. In all cases, and this is what we wish to emphasise, the dream highlights the trait or the quality carried by a person with whom the dreamer identifies on this very point. The dream works on the identification which is always identification with a trait. It allows the dreamer to isolate and reflect on his/her position with regard to this drive trait. For the trait itself brings into play a tendency, a pulsional disposition, that is at the origin of the dream. One of the functions of symbols, *via* the figuration, is to make the trait appear, often in several places in the dream, favouring the work on the drive. The term "trait" covers the notion of attribute or quality. It is a representative of the drive, a vector of identification.[19]

Temporality and causality

The division of time into singular moments, outside of temporal seriation, appears frequently in the course of dreams in the form of suspensions in its development. The grasp of the successive and the simultaneous, initially neglected by mythical thought, is replaced by relations of causality; subsequently the category of causality will be differentiated from that of succession and a temporal order instituted. In dreams, on the other hand, by a characteristic inversion of mythical thought, causality is often replaced by succession. The representation of two successive scenes indicates that they are connected by a causal relationship. Where logical thinking, which underlies the principle of causality, begins by identifying elements, mythical thinking does not produce any division or isolation of elements. Change, whether governed by the principle of causality or some other principle, is replaced in mythical thinking by metamorphosis and redundant in dreams.

For Freud, the transformation of "thoughts" into visual images is related to the regression[20] in the dream process during which the investment follows a retrograde path. The representation returns to the traces of perception—the sensory images from which it originates. For Freud, this regressive movement is triggered by the attraction of a visual memory that seeks to be actualised. The Freudian concept makes the dream the substitute of an infantile scene, modified by the transference into a recent domain. Actually, the scene is not always infantile and not necessarily modified into a recent domain. But the regression is both topical and temporal and also formal since primitive modes of expression, such as symbols, are used. The transformation of "thoughts" into visual images merely follows, in reverse, the path which, starting from perception, led to thought and is represented in its primitive mythical form by dreams.

Notes

1 J. Lassègue, Une réinterprétation de la notion de forme symbolique dans un scénario récent d'émergence de la culture (A reinterpretation of "symbolic form" in a recent storyline of the emerging of culture), *Revue de métaphysique et de morale*, 2007/2, no. 54.
2 E. Cassirer, *Philosophy of Symbolic Forms, Volume 1, Language,* Routledge, 2020.
3 Muriel van Vliet, Art et langage chez Ernst Cassirer: morphologie et/ou structuralisme (Art and language in Ernst Cassirer: morphology and/or structuralism), in *Images Re-vues, Histoire, anthropologie et théorie de l'art*, Hors-série, 5, 2016.
4 E. Cassirer, *Liberté et forme, L'idée de la culture alllemande* (Freedom and Form: the German idea of culture), Paris, Les éditions du cerf, 2001. Translated by us.
5 E. Cassirer, *Philosophy of Symbolic Forms, Volume II, Mythic Thought,* Routledge, 2020.
6 This theme is close to Jungian thought and to the experience recounted in *The Red Book* except that at the end of this experience God has lost his absolute character. Schelling is one of Jung's references.
7 *Ibid.*
8 The persistence of mythical differentiations of space and their articulation with the divine world is the principle of the constitution of the anterior and posterior realms of God in President Schreber's delusion. *Freud-Jung Letters, op. cit.*
9 *Ibid.*
10 E. Cassirer, *Language and Myth,* Dover Publications. Inc., New York, 1953.
11 This remark seems to us to be very important with regard to the persistence of mythical thought and the constant work that language must carry out to free itself from it.
12 *Ibid.*
13 R. Otto, *The Idea of the Holy,* Oxford University Press, 1923.
14 *Ibid.*
15 This is one of the points of the Freud-Jung debate. Have logical relations been suspended because of censorship or have they not yet been constructed? For Jung, "logical" thought is thought in words. "Analogical" thought is thought in images.
16 S. Freud, *The Unconscious* (1915), SE, Vol. XIV.
17 The interpretation of the dream requires the identification of these points of contact.
18 S. Freud. *The Interpretation of Dreams, op. cit.* Chapter VI, The Work of the Dream.
19 In French, the term "trait" brings up the equivocation with the line in writing and is the basis of the Lacanian concept of unary trait. It is both a feature, a quality and the mark of the subject as "one", referring to the *einziger Zug* of Freud and his concept of identification. This term trait is also used to speak of primary identification, but at this stage, the first mark of the subject is a trait that could be said to be without qualities.
20 *Ibid.* Chapter VII, Psychology of Dreams.

Bibliography

Cassirer, E., *Language and myth*, Dover Publications Inc, New-York, 1953.

Cassirer, E., *Liberté et forme, L'idée de la culture alllemande*, Les éditions du cerf, Paris, 2001.

Cassirer, E., *The philosophy of symbolic forms*, Volume 1, Language, Routledge, 2020.

Cassirer, E., *The philosophy of symbolic forms*, Volume 2, Mythic Thought, Routledge, 2020.

Freud, S., *The interpretation of dreams*, Vol. IV–V, SE, 1900.

Freud, S., *The Unconscious*, Vol. XIV, SE, 1915.

Lassègue, J., Une réinterprétation de la notion de forme symbolique dans un scénario récent d'émergence de la culture, Revue de métaphysique et de morale, 2007/2, no. 54.

The Freud-Jung Letters, ed. W. Mc Guire, Princeton University Press, 1974.

Otto, R., *The idea of the Holy*, Oxford University Press, 1923.

van Vliet, M., Art et langage chez Ernst Cassirer: morphologie et/ou structuralisme, Images Re-vues, Histoire, anthropologie et théorie de l'art, Hors-série, 5, 2016.

Chapter 4

The work of the letter

The transcription of dreams inscribes the traces of transference. It is the transference that gives rise to dreams and guides the analyst's transcription. It is the transcription that makes it possible, when rereading the dreams afterwards to identify the repetition, to highlight what is repeated before being connected. It is indeed repetition, as repetition of the subject, repetition of marks of the subject, that sets in. A thread, several threads are woven from one dream to another. It is his work, a linking and unlinking work operated within the dream itself but also in following dreams, by the Freudian trio: figuration, displacement and condensation, that we call the *work of the letter*.[1] The transcription of dreams only could highlight this aspect, though it was predictable considering the relationship of the subject to the language. However, the transcription of dreams sheds considerable light on the structure but above all on the constitution of the main signifiers of the subject, in neurosis and just as much in psychosis.

Displacement–condensation

Our understanding of the work of the letter is based on the linchpin of dreams, the Freudian displacement–condensation pairing, in addition to figurability. Condensation brings together *identical or similar elements.* Dreams draw attention to these points of similarity recorded by the dreamer, though unaware of them when awakened. These points of similarity bring together what was perceived unconsciously. It is this similarity that is expressed in a symbolic way. As in mythical thinking, condensation matches elements according to similarities to create new entities. The displacement is a displacement of investment: a latent element is replaced by another more distant one. But the displacement is not the sole fact of censorship. The psychic accent, the value, is in the forefront. The displacement represents the movement of thought that proceeds by successive trial and error. Dreams are an indicator of the moving of the investment, transferring itself from one "object" to another one in order to search and name as precisely as possible. The displacement is equivalent to metonymy, it is a new naming, according to the etymology of the term. The name emphasises a

DOI: 10.4324/b23380-5

particular aspect of the object and it is on this particularity that the value of the name lies. The identification of a feature is therefore inseparable from its naming. Through the successive differentiations and naming it produces, metonymy is the motor of the development of dreams in series.

The term letter refers to the processes of deciphering-cyphering or reading-writing of dreams. Before "writing" in its specific pictorial way, dreams "read". They read from the trace, reactivated by the day residues, little events from the previous day's life that have held the dreamer back without his/her knowledge and have challenged him/her on a instinctual level. These day residues call forth other traces, traces that are both mnemonic and instinctual, signs of perception, according to Freud's diagram.[2] These traces are the mark of a instinctual experience that could not be put into words, a coincidence between pending linguistic elements and a strong instinctual investment that froze them. The regression of dreams makes these traces able to be reached. Regression, this capacity to reach an otherwise inaccessible material, gives dreams their specificity, their value as a unique tool. But in order to be read, these traces require the reading apparatus that constitutes the work of the dream and the appearance of the images that will call for words. In this respect, dreams constitute a modality of treatment of the drive, it is an apparatus for reading the drive traces, thanks to symbols. Dreams are triggered by a piece of real, not symbolised yet. Let us note that the only affect likely to be brought into play in dreams is anguish, a sign of the imminence of the real. This piece of real arouses an instinctual response that has remained unrepresented until then. Dreams work to produce symbolisation of this piece of real, providing symbols as images, then words. It is the work of the dream in the transference that allows this response, the elaboration of a chain, a knotting, in any case a link between certain linguistic elements that will then, but only then, be able to access the status of signifiers.

The dream series

The symbolic forms, as Cassirer understands them, develop in one piece, from mythical to scientific thought, with a special place reserved for language as a mediator in the specification of the different forms. His understanding implies that the boundaries between "objective" and "subjective" are not immutably defined, on the contrary. The general concept of objectivity is based entirely on the disjunction of the elements of experience and the critical work of the mind, which separates the essential from the accidental, the variable from the permanent and the contingent from the necessary. What distinguishes the perceptual awareness of an object from the scientific awareness of that object is a difference of degree, not of kind. The distinctions of value present in the former will be elevated in the latter to the form of knowledge and fixed *via* the concept and the judgement.

Myths live in a world of figures that emerge as something objective. Myths are born of emotion, it is caught up in affect, but an affect that is not aware of itself and that blurs the boundaries between subject and object. The crisis that gives rise to empirical and conceptual knowledge has not yet taken place. The intensity with which the object assaults consciousness and takes possession of it does not allow it to enlarge this moment, to unite it with another one, with a past or a future, to make it an element of a series. What is missing is a stable border between representation and perception, between wish and its fulfilment and between image and thing. This world without borders is indeed the one that dreams stage, but it is also this world that the analysis of the dream and especially that of its seriation will limit and circumscribe.

The identification of similarities is already one of the functions of dreams and at the principle of condensation, as we have seen. The transcription of the dreams highlights the organisation of the dreams into series around certain words or even around certain themes. Several series progress at the same time to intersect at a certain number of points. It is therefore not one element that pursues a serial development but several elements evolving together and presenting relationships between them, permanent relationships that are present from the beginning to the end. These relationships evolve in accordance with constant progression but with moments of opposition, of inversion, typical of the symbolic function. The progression of these elements is subject to fixed principles, it obeys a law ordering the seriation and the intersection of series. Through the creation specific to dreams, elements that seemed separate are ordered into series, according to a stable configuration, governed by principles. The implementation of a law of development can be inferred from the structural analogies between the different sequences. Every creation is in some way a recreation of the previous one.

Gathering elements in the form of a series presupposes a common element that is specified in the various elements of the series, that manifests itself in all of them but in each of them with a nuance, a difference of its own. This common element concerns a piece of real, a trace which is called to symbolisation and repeated in different forms linked together. The setting up of this structure of repetition is the sign of the work on the drive carried out by dreams. A repetition, but then a signifying repetition takes place, takes the place of what was, until then, a compulsion to repeat, induced by a real not symbolised yet, an acting out excluding the subject. Repetition becomes signifying because it connects elements through the progression inherent in series, but also through elements belonging to different series which connect themselves through them.

This signifying repetition is the index of the process of reading the trace, indicating a process on the way, through the transformation of the traces into traits, carried by symbols. The enciphering and deciphering work of dreams produce the traits but requires an intermediary phase, a preparatory phase, a transit through the image and the symbol, the bearer and vehicle of the trait. The progression of dreams reveals the serial structure that underlies it, a rhizome structure of which each dream constitutes a point of emergence.

This network is organised around a central hole. The elaboration of each dream, in fact, remains constantly unfinished. It finds its limit in a point of abutment, where the associations stop, revealing the constitutive incompleteness of the symbolic apparatus on which each dream is moored. This incompleteness is translated by the Freudian notion of the dream's umbilicus. The process of symbolisation nevertheless continues, but to do so requires a new point of emergence, a new dream. Dreams, in a sense, constantly rework the same figures, transforming them and adding new elements. Metamorphosis, characteristic of dreams, is constantly present. But, because of the organisation of dreams into series, metamorphosis in the Goethean sense, a group of transformations, takes precedence over metamorphosis in the Ovidian sense, which, until then, signalled the rupture, the elision of the link between one form and another, a link that the seriation of dreams, on the contrary, restores and privileges. The symbolic function works in two stages; the first stage produces symbols, which are vectors of traits, and the second stage initiates the seriation of traits.

Clinic

The specificity of psychonalysis in relation to other human sciences is that it is based on clinical experience, which cannot be dissociated from its theorisation. We consider it essential to give an overview of the clinical expression of the processes of symbolisation as we have outlined them above. We need to show how these processes are expressed individually. Dreams are anonymous products which do not contravene the reserve required in the analytical field while showing the development of symbolisation, its continuity and its stages. Clinical experience bears witness to the dynamics of a process, a movement that must be identified.

Dreams connect to the past but for the construction of a present desire, supporting itself with a new language, a renewed language, produced by the work of myth through language. It is thus a question of identifying the modifications of a group of transformations. Under the impulse of the transference, as a result of the encounter with the Other, the process of symbolisation, immobilised, frozen and fixed, is set in motion again and prepares a new response to the shock that generated the fixation. From then on, we need to follow the thread of dream productions, organised into series of dreams, starting from the different elements attached to the point of fixation. These series will follow their own path and then intersect and bring together elements that were previously disjointed. Or, on the contrary, in other structural organisations, they will individualise, starting from points of condensation, mythical formations, to take distinct paths.

Recently, several studies reported progress in the treatment of psychotic patient in which dreams were playing a leading role; they were a lever in the cure progression. Apollo, Bergeron and Cantin, a group from Quebec,[3]

C. Kolko[4] in France, Celeste Labaronnie[5] in Argentina reported such cases. We drew attention to this point in 1992[6] already, with the case of A. which theory has been completed ever since.

It is the same material which is reorganised by dreams and delusion, but the difference is significant, it concerns the place left on the subject. The transfer of this material from delusion to dreams is what will allow the subject to recognise them as his/her own. While delusion vanishes, dreams come up gradually. Transference starts digging a breach in delusion and opening a rift, a hole. This hole is a hole in the language, testifying the symbolic incompleteness and its boundaries revealed by dreams themselves. It is the same hole, seen but rejected, which is covered by delusion. Indeed, it is not the knowledge gained from his experience of the hole in the language but the solution that the psychotic patient works to produce that causes the disease. Faced to the default of language, the psychotic patient responds with an unconscious mission, a kind of repair mission, that is producing a complete world. It is this flaw, reopened by transference, that dreams will come and edge with their literal elements.

The signifiers of dreams are the very ones which have been caught up in delusion, but dreams link them in a new way. This new link, a signifying link, since series of dreams are implementing chains of signifiers, is what allows us to talk about analytic treatment of psychosis and not just stabilisation. Dreams mobilise the frozen elements and develop them. They awaken traces, not transformed into words yet, by their specific action which proceed from images that themselves call words. The cure progresses this way. Then the dream work will bring together one or more memories that were essentials by the time the psychosis itself was established. Dreams thus engage a process of recollection, replacing these memories in the subject personal story.

Primary identification, a first trait

Dreams are triggered by a point of appeal, that of real, an instinctual trace, non-represented yet. Dreams work to produce symbolisation at this very point, starting again from this trace. In psychosis, transference functions as a verification apparatus authenticating in language an impression, an impression that has remained outside language, or rather outside speech, foreclosed. Clinically, transference gives rise to a series of dreams on the same matrix, as in A.

The series

With A., hallucinations gave way as soon as dreams progress. It is this movement of *substitution of dreams for hallucinations* that attracted our attention and led us to systematically transcribe his dreams. Noticing, afterwards, the organisation of the dreams in series, brought us to identify several sequences revolving around key elements. These sequences overlapped. At their intersection, major dreams turned out to have a knotting function, a padding function.

In A., several series could be individualised. These series revolve around:

* The hole. His first occurrence in dreams was a hole that appeared in his bedroom door. This dream preceded a crisis, an acute delusional episode that required hospitalisation. Later, after the crisis, the hole took the form of a gash, a cut and then a wound, as successive metonymies of the hole.

* The body. In following dreams these holes and cuts circulated and hung on to different points of the body.

* The letter. School dreams appeared during which he made dictations, essays, dissertations, he wrote.

* A fourth series consisted of the recurring presence of a paternal character, father or grandfather.

Tying of series

These four series were then tied together in a padding dream that we called *the dream of the circumflex accent*:

My grandfather looks at me. I am told: "Something is *missing*". I draw a circumflex under his eyebrows.

It should be noted that it is following the call of "something missing" that the accent is inscribed. Another dream follows: He has blood in his eyebrows. This latter dream brings up a memory, the memory of a bandage worn by him in his early childhood, on this part of his body, above his eyebrows. This bandage was in fact intended to protect his forehead. Protection was necessary because of repeated and unexplained falls on his head. His father, keen on photography, often pictured him wearing the bandage. His father's "photographic" gaze reappeared in the dream, attributed to his grandfather.

But for this dream to occur, the previous dreams had to make prior substitutions. The hole is re-named, became a gash, then a wound and moved to different points on the body, finally settling on the eyebrows. The eyebrow condensed the point of impact of the wound, where the bandage was placed, and the accent that underlined the grandfather's gaze. The grandfather himself is condensed with the father, that is how the father took his picture. This point can be linked to its hallucinatory form: "*Pictures were blinking at me*", he said after the crisis that briefly interrupted the treatment. It is this point of real that dreams would later write.

In dreams, something is written, this is our thesis, which limits the drive, which circumscribes it with the effect of stopping the hallucinatory emergence. The knotting of the body to the letter is contemporary with the observation of lacking, realised there in the form of the missing accent: "The circumflex accent is missing". The circumflex accent, a letter, then takes the place of the lacking. It comes to circumscribe the gaze where the wound stood.

It is only starting from the dream of the circumflex accent that condensation manifests. The following dream, the dream of the blood in the eyebrows, brings in association the childhood memory of the headband protecting his forehead. This memory brings up the necessary element, it brings up the element that enables the condensation to be read and the ciphered element that is the eyebrow, to be deciphered. Why the eyebrow? Because it is the place of the wound. The eyebrow that is his grandfather's in the dream, turns out to be also, deciphered by the association, his own eyebrow, the one that wore the headband. The association brings the second element that makes possible the reading of the first. During the crisis, pictures blinked at him. The dream of the circumflex accent leads to the re-emergence and the subjectivisation of material previously present in the delusion. Following the last two dreams, he came to notice the equivocality of language. "Words had materialised", he said.

Let us now return to Lacan, his upside-down bouquet and the seminar on transference, mentioned in Chapter 2. In the montage of the inverted bouquet, the eye symbolises the subject, but for the knotting of the imaginary to the real to take place correctly, the eye must be suitably situated, i.e. the position made for the subject in the symbolic must be sufficiently assured. Let us recall that, for this model of the inverted bouquet, Lacan referred to the optical instrument summoned in the *Interpretation of Dreams* by Freud, himself led by this observation: the transformation, specific to dreams, of thought into visual images. In order to see oneself properly in the mirror, *the relation to the totem*, to the dead father, that is to say to the superego and the Ego-ideal, must be internalised. This passage from the outside to the inside is achieved by the introjection of the superego via the totemic meal. It is the dialectic of introjection that produces the turn from the superego, external, to the Ego-ideal, internal and narcissistic, sufficiently narcissistic to be an object of libidinal investment for the subject. The dream is the motor of this introjection. So, in summary: "Pictures were blinking at me", said A., after the crisis, "My grandfather is looking at me", he dreamed later.

Metaphorisation: from the hole in the door to the circumflex

Primordial identification is identification with a trait of the object, with a sign of the Other, the one towards which the subject in the mirror turns to assure himself of who he is. The subject internalises the gaze of the other via a sign, a sign of the Other's assent: a single trait. It is enough for the subject to coincide, in the mirror, in his relationship with the Other, so that he can dispose of this sign. "I draw above his eyebrows a circumflex accent", the dream said. This circumflex accent irresistibly evokes the metaphor "eyebrows in a circumflex accent", although it is not mentioned by the patient.

Metaphor, the substitution of a signifier for another, is not a symbol. Symbols are constructed on the basis of a trait of similarity with the object. This trait of similarity is also present in metaphor, whatever Lacan said[7] and it is not to be neglected. It is indeed on this basis, similarity, that dreams are constructed. This trait is the basis of substitution, but in the case of metaphor, which distinguishes it from symbol, it is the substitution of a signifier for another. As such, it produces an effect, it impacts the drive. Metaphor is preceded by a comparison; it always presupposes an image which is the most primitive figure. But the metaphor differs from the simile in that one of its terms is removed. The element that denotes the comparison, the "as" or the "as if" is removed.

In A., this metaphor is not pronounced. It is not until the following dream that the proper dimension of the signifier is revealed for him. This accent that encircles the gaze, borders it, circumscribes it, is here, and this is the continuation of our thesis, the unary trait that signs, via the Other, the identification of the subject. He then disposes of this trait, and as proof, he produces a second dream on the same matrix, the dream of the blood in the eyebrows. This dream, an exceptional fact for this subject in whom associations are practically non-existent, produces the emergence of a memory, that of the photographer father, and of himself as the subject of the photograph, wearing the famous eyebrow band. It is from this point onwards that: "Words are materialised". Words take on a personal, physical meaning. The equivocality of language appears to him, it appears at the point where the mythical thought disappears. The transference confronts the subject with the incompleteness of the symbolic and its consequences. This incompleteness can be compared to the "death of the father", a death that can be as real as in A., whose troubles broke out shortly afterwards, or any event with similar symbolic value.

The unary trait

We don't know what exactly happened in A.'s early childhood, we don't know what caused him to fall on his head repeatedly. His mother told him that his head was too heavy. In any case, at some point perhaps, knowledge could not be faulted. It was taken at face value and no thinking was possible. The establishment of the transference allowed the validation of a knowledge inhabited by the subject, that is to say, the equivalent of an authorisation to think. Through the effect of the transference, the displacement of the trace on the stage of dreams could then occur. The consequence of this displacement was the erasure of the trace, that is, its passage through symbols to the status of sign and then to that of signifier. From a trace implying a desire and the passage of a subject, the subject comes to impose its own mark, that is, its reading of the trace, which goes hand in hand with its erasure.[8] This is the sign, in a way, of the mourning of this flawless knowledge that could not be put in default. It is only insofar as it can designate something potentially missing that a *quality can become significant.* As far as A. is concerned, this lacking is not just any lacking, it is the lacking in initiating the symbolic function. This function inscribes incompleteness as inherent in the symbolic order and allows the advent of significance as the trademark of this lacking within language itself.[9] This is what happened for A. The words took shape, he perceived the equivocity of language. A first point of mooring of the body to language was now fixed. This point was thus correlative to the assumption of the incompleteness of the symbolic, that is, of a lacking in the Other that the letter circumscribes.

In A.'s case, the succession of dreams realised series operating by successive substitutions. In his case, the substitutions concerned perforations on different points of the body and finally located on the eyebrow with the dream of the circumflex accent. We have underlined the importance of the circumflex accent, which stigmatised the emergence of the letter's line on this point of the body. The line of the letter comes to outline the drive. At first, the succession of dreams seems to be governed only by displacement or, if one prefers, metonymy, which we take in its etymological sense of new nomination. The body, which at the beginning is only apprehended as an undifferentiated whole, pars pro toto, or toto pro pars, becomes the object of successive discriminations, in series, with the concomitant nomination of the different points of the body. It is only from the dream of the circumflex accent that condensation begins. It is there that we situate a knotting, a padding point. It is there that the trait comes out, a trait that could support the identification of the subject. What seems remarkable here is that condensation can only happen after a prior work of the metonymic function, a prior work of nomination. It is this work of nomination that, relying on a lacking, triggers metaphorisation, a signifying metaphorisation at present.

The treatment of psychosis progresses through the different stages involved in the implementation of the symbolic function. The reinvestment of these traces awaiting symbolisation is the first stage. It is the transference that allows this reinvestment from which dreams result. The second stage concerns the constitution of traits representing the subject. Metonymy comes to organise the displacements and the related nominations, producing several signifying series, advancing in concert and then crossing each other to finally establish a network structure, itself a condition for the appearance of the subject and the emergence of signifiance, of the equivocity proper to language. Seriation is contemporary with the advent of the subject and the marking of its productions with its own seal.

The one and the many

Jung, through the dream narratives of his autobiography and the testimony of the *Red Book*, provided us with the material for another clinical case. Jung maintained a closeness to mythic thinking for several reasons. His experience of schizophrenia, alongside Eugen Bleuler, enabled him to grasp its specific hyper symbolism and to relate it to myths. Moreover, Jung's personal history as a pastor's son also made him sensitive to the place of religion in man and to the attachment of religion to its mythical roots. As Cassirer showed it, the emergence of the sense of self accompanied the advent of the religious stage which followed the progress of mythic consciousness. The divine, first connected to objects, to activities, then personified with its attributes, was finally reduced to the One, devoid of properties but also of name. The concrescence of mythical thought implied the denial of differences and the constitution of a plurality of distinct beings. It only recognised an alternative relationship between the one and the many, equating the many with the one or the one with the many. But as the objects of human action became more diverse, the unity of the acting subject itself emerged more and more clearly, produced by its opposite, the plurality of forms of action. The journey from the mythical to the religious went hand in hand with that of consciousness, which grasped itself as one, in the face of a God who was less and less particularised.

As we have seen, it is also this journey from the mythical to the religious that Jung retraced in his own way in his theoretical work. For him, the collective unconscious is a residue from an undifferentiation from the Other, a mythical residue, a lack of differentiation material in the state of traces, that must be developed. In the absence of development, this material would be projected in the way of mythical thought. It would be destined to projection, to "divine" projection. The projection of the Ideal founds the psychological essence of the notion of God and it results in the establishment of the religious function. For Jung, God is a psychic instance, it is a projection of the self. This projection is the basis of mystical participation, according to the term borrowed from Lévy-Bruhl, the residue of a lack of differentiation between the subject and the object characterising primitive mentality. Jung understood the essential role of projection in the relationship between man and the divine, determining the future of its residue: mystical participation. According to Jung, three paths are possible[10]:

1 Mystical participation. It thus consists of the projection of the Ideal in the form of the God/father. It is the sign of the persistence of the residue of subject/object a lack of differentiation, typical of mythical thought. It constitutes the middle way, the one used by the neurosis with its father/God put in the position of Ideal.
2 Withdrawal from projection. The withdrawal of projection and the introjection of the divine image exposes the danger of inflation and dissolution of the personality by identification with the unconscious, what Jung calls ordinary madness. If the projection is withdrawn and reintegrated as it is into the ego, this process will result in identification with the unconscious and the narcissistic inflation characteristic of psychosis.

3   The overcoming (of projection). The abolition of *mystical participation*, making room for the unconscious. This is the way of the synthesis of opposites. Projection is not reintegrated but elaborated by the way of dreams realising the synthesis of opposites, *via* symbols. God becomes this residual God from whom this remnant of primitive lack of differentiation, the source of projection, has been removed. *The overcoming presupposes that the projection, as an emanation of narcissism, is reintegrated and subjectivised through dreams and symbols.* God becomes the Other, a plurality made up of pairs of opposites, *imprinting the mark of its structure on the transference, a plural and no longer dual structure, a collective structure.*

This third outcome describes what happened to Jung himself, the outcome of the crisis brought about by the break with Freud. The question of the relationship to the God/Father was opened up in the transference to Freud, brought about by dreams, a series of dreams about the awakening of the dead.[11] Then, the rupture triggered the crisis and its visions and finally its resolution through the writing of *The Red Book*.[12] In its final part, *The Seven Sermons to the Dead,* Philemon just addresses the dead, in a discourse on the constitution of the divine world and the development of a conception of the unconscious.

The point of view of the *Sermons* is precisely that of the manifestation of the divine in the created world. As we have seen, *The seven sermons* refer to the notion of the Pleroma, borrowed from Gnostic systems. The Pleroma is conceived as *a primordial unconscious,* a proto-inconscious articulating the links between the divine world and the Creature through the notion of *quality* which is a prefiguration of the Jungian archetype. This elaboration is the product of the crisis that Jung went through and constitutes one of the pillars of its resolution.

The Pleroma is made up of all the qualities that make up the divine world, but the latter does not have qualities in itself. In the Pleroma, in fact, the archetypal qualities coexist in a fused state, as simple possibilities of structuring. The qualities, organised in pairs of opposites, cancel each other out because of their opposition. The Creature, on the other hand, is the manifested face of the Pleroma, as the necessary reflection of the One in the many. The Creature, unlike the Pleroma, possesses qualities that are differentiated and separate from each other. Its task is to perceive and bring into existence *the qualities of the Pleroma, distinct traits,* which constitute pairs of opposites. The world of symbols results on the union, on the bringing together of contrary elements in a middle way that is not a compromise but a transformation of the original elements. Symbolic knowledge is a direct intuition of the ontological reality of the object to be known. Things are first known in their pleromatical, undifferentiated state. The process of individuation, the differentiation which is the task of the Creature, is the result of the integration of the knowledge carried by symbols. The *principium individuationis* is the instrument of a first differentiation that brings all things, all qualities, into existence, so that the individual consciousness that perceives them can distinguish itself from them by carrying out the second differentiation, the withdrawal of the projections into the objects.

Jung takes myth in reverse and returns to its roots. Man could *only* apprehend his action on *condition that he projected it outside, and it is from this projection that the figure of the god was born*. The Jungian conception is close to that of Usener, as reported by Cassirer. As we have seen, the sacred does not indicate an attribute specific to the object but a mode of relation to this object, impersonal and anonymous. Myths passed from the first anonymous phase to the exact opposite phase, the phase of polysemy. The personal god gathered in himself a host of attributes which were those of the special gods whose union he brought about. Including in himself the attributes of these gods, he also took their names. Finally, with the unity of the concept of god, which can no longer be designated by any name, the divine becomes a being without properties, since any property would limit its own essence; it excludes all particular attributes in order to draw its predicates only from itself.

In the conception of the unconscious as a Pleroma, the attributes of the divine are present but neutralised, because they are fused and therefore inoperative. It is the task of the Creature to produce their differentiation and to make them exist by perceiving them. The Creature, that is to say, the subject, perceives, differentiates and brings into existence the qualities of the Pleroma in the form of pairs of opposites, and in doing so, detaches itself from it. It extracts itself from the divine and is only in relation with what remains of it, symbols. This is what the effectiveness of the individuation process, as experienced by Jung himself and as a prototype for the work to come, consists of. The discrimination of qualities brings them into existence and this is what produces the separation between the subject and the divine Other and even, more broadly, the separation between the subject and the Other.

This identification of the traits of the Other, which undoes its omnipotence, is also the cornerstone of the treatment of psychoses; it is the lever of the subjectivisation process, as we saw it in A. The Jungian conception is, as we said, below the formation of the symptom. It avoids it by withdrawing the projection of the divine ideal and integrating the opposites. It is by another route that symptom is formed.

The symptom, a mythical residue

The Freudian re-elaboration of *Totem and Taboo*, the first occurrence of identification with a trait through the relationship to the totem, the ancestor, produced *Collective Psychology and Ego Analysis*. The setting up of the Ego-ideal confirmed the link to the father as to repression and symptom, as well as to the organisation in crowds. The symptom itself bears the mark, the imprint of its prehistory. The totem of the phobia presents the emblem of the drive,

the taboo of the obsessed person retains one of the branches of the antagonistic couple nourishing his/her ambivalence, the body of the hysteric figures
that could not be put into words. Phobia, obsessive neurosis and hysteria,
each in its own way, testify to the survival of the primitive time of myth.

Let us return to the symbolism of the symptom and the notion of mnemic
symbol. The memic symbol is connected to the formation of the symptom, as
associated with the traumatic event and a symbol of this event. Introduced by
Freud in relation to hysteria, this notion disappears and then reappears in
Inhibition, Symptom and Anxiety. The mnemic symbol[13] is a result of
repression, a kind of encysted foreign body, incapable of binding with other
elements of the same nature. The symptom is the symbol of the trauma, but
deprived of its symbolic efficiency, that of associating with other symbols. The
symptom is defined as the substitute and the sign of a drive satisfaction that
has not taken place. The expected pleasure of satisfaction is transformed by
the process of repression into unpleasantness, anguish. The anxiety is not
produced during repression but expresses, in the form of the affect, a pre-
existing mnemic image. The affect, which is incorporated into the psychic life
as a sediment of very old traumatic events, is recalled in similar situations as a
mnemic symbol. The mnemic symbol, which determines the specificity of the
symptom, is very close to the *notion of mnemonic trace,* itself a condition of
possibility for the conservation and transfer of excitation.

Hans[14] is anxiously awaiting an event: the horse will bite him. There is a
conflict of ambivalence between love and hate towards the father, for which the
phobia is an attempt at a solution. The reinforcement of one of the branches,
resulting in the excessive and compulsive character of tenderness (reaction-
formation), could have been another solution but it is not used by Hans. The
phobia is the heir to the motion of hatred against the father and the fear of his
revenge, castration. The fear of retaliation is normal, what in fact characterises
the neurosis is this one and only point: *the substitution of the horse for the father.*
What favours this displacement is the survival of *innate traces of totemic
mentality,* which can, at this young age, be activated.[15] The instinctual impulse,
hostile to the father, has been repressed by the process of transformation into
its opposite and, in place of the aggression against the father, the aggression of
the father towards him appears. The representation of the devouring by the
father[16] could be the degraded expression of the tender motion, a passive
tender motion that would represent the desire to be loved by the father in the
sense of genital eroticism. Not only one but two instinctual impulses are
concerned—sadistic aggression against the father and passive tenderness towards him—and form *a pair of opposites.* The formation of the phobia also
suppresses the tender object investment in the mother.

The anguish, constituting the essence of the phobia, does not originate in
the repression process nor in the libidinal investments of the repressed impulses, but is the agent of repression. The anxiety of the animal phobia is
castration anxiety, an anxiety in front of a real or at least judged real danger.

It is the anxiety that produces the repression, and not the repression that produces the anxiety. In this case, as in all cases where sexual excitation is inhibited, the libido is transformed into anguish. It is in order to avoid the dangerous situation indicated by the development of anxiety that the symptom is formed. The formation of the symptom has the result of suppressing the situation of danger. It has two sides: one, hidden, has made it possible to escape the danger, the other, apparent, shows what has been created in place of the instinctual impulse, namely, the substitute formation, the phobia. The phobia is emblematic of the constitution of symbols. The danger is an instinctual danger.

However, Freud actually emphasises the consequences of this danger, namely, in Hans' case, the father's reaction of revenge, instead of the danger itself. This leads to a projection of what is in fact an instinctual danger to the outside, as if the danger did not come from within but from outside. It is indeed because the father does not respond, or not as he should, that there is an appeal to this singular symbolic element, crystallising as Lacan says, making up for the failure of this zero symbolic value that is the Name-of-the-Father or symbolic father. In place of the trait, the totem itself appears, carrying the trait of the drive that ordered the identification. As Laplanche points out,[17] if the horse can be considered as a substitute for the father, we could also consider this same horse as having come to arbitrarily bind an affect that without it would wreak havoc.

Is the choice of horse arbitrary? Hans gives explanations[18]: it is of such and such a colour, it falls, it moves its legs and it bites. So it is not the father or even the mother, it is *this or that trait* of the father or mother or of the subject himself, which presentifies the instinctual danger and which the symbol, carrier of several of these traits, embodies. The horse symbol carries a combination of traits that can be associated and dissociated at any time. In Hans, moreover, the characteristics of the phobia change: the fear that the horse will bite him becomes a compulsion to look at horses, a fear that horses will fall, a fear of the black on their mouths, etc. It is also an indication of the re-launch of the symbolisation process and the progress of the treatment, splitting the symbol-totem into each of the features in which the drive has come to be incarnated. The mythical, concrete and globalising thought that produced the totem-horse is replaced by the differentiation of its attributes, which are themselves the carriers of the instinctual dangers that the family configuration was unable to curb and that the analytical work will partially circumscribe.

Symbolisation can bring together two representations or two modalities of relationship but it can also link an affect and a representation. The binding of representations together is achieved by the energy that flows along their connections. Energy, investment and affect are terms that can be paralleled. If there is a change in the flow of energy, the connection becomes fixed and the affect is stuck in place, immobilised, in a dead-end system. The liberation of the affect then requires the creation of new configurations, i.e. the restarting of the symbolisation process. *In fact, the effectiveness of the liberation of the affect lies in the creation of a new configuration of symbols.*

Hans' horse is a signifier-symbol, "recrystallising" and solving the problem in its own way, at the cost of the symptom, in this case the phobia. The symptom is first of all a symbol, but isolated, not chained. Its deciphering and the resulting chaining only will make it a signifier.

Reading the symptom with the symbol

Symbols are required in a situation of rupture or confrontation. A situation whose contradictions cannot be worked out produces the eclipse of the subject. The subject is absent from the event, of which only traces remain, the Freudian signs of perception. The trauma produces a subjective absence and the remaining traces need to be first translated into images. Symbols encode the pending traces, inscribing them in the form of images and waiting for a subject to read them.

The symptom conflict is a battle between opposing forces. In the case of a psychic conflict between two representations, the formation of a mnemic symbol takes the place of the repressed representation. Symbols bear witness to the trauma and *keep fixed*, in the form of the symptom, as long as the contradiction from which it results remains. The strength of the instinctual impulse can produce the reversal of the drive into its opposite, as an exteriorisation of the repression. From then on, the reversal into its opposite governs the shaping of the symptom. In dreams, opposition and contradiction do not appear as such. Only one element of the pair of opposites is privileged and figured and the reversal is revealed only by the analysis of the dream.

To free the fixation of the symptom, symbols are irreplaceable. It is thanks to symbols that the repressed branch of the pair of opposites reappears and allows their confrontation. Where the symptom has privileged one of the pair of opposites, symbols will, by their very function, restore the other, the repressed branch of the conflict underlying a drive trait. *In a way, symbols, as mediation, oppose the reversionary movement of the drive from which the symptom often originates.*

Let's take the study of B.'s dreams as an example. They can be broken down into several series.

- A series of numbers: 1, 2, 3.
- A series of colours: green, blue, white, black, brown and chocolate. These colours carry a symbolism that is present in culture, white for purity, black for death … . The last two, brown, chocolate, denote, in French, a loss, in this particular case, directly named by language. Language uses the symbolism of colour in its own symbolic form, by forging a qualifier.
- A series of objects: clothes, shoes, cars, bags, fruits.

B. is the second of two siblings. She lost her mother at the age of two following a miscarriage. She was born at a "bad time" for her mother, a bad time that death freezes into an endless mourning. This will leave a trace visible in her dreams, in the form of the number two. These two are, first of all, twice the same, a pair that returns repeatedly in dreams, like a count that cannot go beyond, something that is repeated before or in order to be able to signify itself. The cure is introduced by a first dream:

She plays the role of one of the seven characters in a children's story. The one in the middle is green, he/she is an undead. On either side of him/her are three other children. Three children, two sets of three, plus one, the one who was never born, the undead with whom she identifies in the dream. *One, two, or three*, these are the numbers around which the treatment will revolve.

A second dream features two twin duets: *two pairs B. + C.* (another woman) confronted with a desired object, an ivory garment that would replace another darker one. In the following dreams, number two marks feet, *two feet* stuck in the same shoe but coming off. The shoe is a fetish object, B. collects them. Then, number two marks houses, *two* very different *houses*, but mirrored, which refer to B. and a colleague, both wearing the same shoes, with one difference, the colour, *white* for one, *blue* for the other. Colour is *the vector of difference. Black* follows, it is the colour of the underwear she wears in an incestuous scene, it is also the colour of the mourning that links her to her mother.

A dream of an abortion then occurs, the loss of the child is signified in these terms: "I am chocolate". Another dream continues the deciphering: "A woman, a professor, embodying knowledge, is also a gynaecologist":

First scene: The gynaecologist cuts the hairs on B's sex. These hairs are very long, recalling a little girl's hair from her childhood; she had very beautiful hair thanks to her mother's care.

Second scene: The gynaecologist tells her that she is pregnant with *twins, a* new occurrence of twice the same.

The first scene is a disillusionment, the bad mother is the one who cuts the hair, cutting the hair is equivalent to removing the breast. But the cut produces a pair. The second scene refers to the father and to sexuality. This cut at the place of sex is equivalent to an oral castration. It brings out the sexual impulses and a fantasy of twin pregnancy. The sexual impulses arise but in the form of an identical pair, *twice the same one*, that we will find in the rest of the dreams.

Then number two marks cars. *Two* different coloured *cars* now appear, one *black*, the other *white*. The desired car, the white one, is worth twice the price of the other. She has bought the black car, the colour of death and of the underwear in the incest dream, instead of the white car, the desired car, which costs double. Black will then be perceived in its value as a masochistic trait of identification with the mother. In another dream, the father beats a child wearing *white* panties. The spanking is correlated with the sexual impulses, but the white here signals the presence of another contradictory current, tenderness.

The dream of the black guard in Converse then unfolds three successive scenes:

In the first scene, a friend is skinny when in reality she is fat. "It's upsetting, like a frustration".

In the second scene, in a restaurant, a "self-service", she has a smaller share than the others, doctors.

In the third scene, the doors of a lift open. A foot appears. A *brown* trainer, a Converse, is on the foot of a *black* guard. He has just had a baby. His father died when he was two. The "Converse" indicates that a conversion is needed. One foot, instead of two, signals the desire to reunite the two parents, the opposites. It also evokes a childhood memory, that of a very nice old lady to whom she used to *kick*. The first scene shows an oral frustration. The second scene develops it: those who have the biggest share are doctors, those who know. The third scene takes up the foot from the dream of the two feet stuck together and separating, but here the foot is unique and refers to the desire to reunite the two parents. It wears a "Converse", something needs to be converted. Moreover, the Converse is brown, it bears the trace of a loss and is associated with it is the memory of kicking the nice lady.

The three reappears, in the form of three *brown* bears, and the staging of a devouring fantasy that is linked to a theft. The theft is referred to a new element, a bag. First a bag, *white* (marriage) on one side, black (death) on the other, then two bags stolen and thrown away. The theft then becomes the theft of a jacket, a symbol of harm in French, which is linked to her sister. It is now the sister, this rival, who is beaten and marked in her body with a colour, blue, which was first the colour of one of the shoes. The father acts as an authority, authority is a problem for B. He reprimands her and she has brought sweets as a sign of guilt. She leaves them, she deprives herself of an oral object.

The oral deprivation resurfaces in the following dream in concerning a fruit soon replaced by a child's garment. This child's garment is at the same time a woman's underwear (dream of incest) replicated *several times* in identical way.

Then occurs *the dream of the blue orange*, born from this fruit that she has deprived herself of: "There is a blue orange. I throw it away. Then an authority claims it from me. This authority is me". The object of deprivation returns in the form of the orange. It is thrown away (like in the dream of the two bags thrown away). The orange is blue, the colour that marked her sister's body, but it is also the colour of her mother's paintings, of seascapes. The blue orange is also related to knowledge, a knowledge that was authoritative and is now rejected: you can paint whatever you want, why not a blue orange.

From the lost and discarded object comes *the dream of the black shoes:* She has given comfortable and elegant black shoes to be repaired. The cobbler can't find them and tells her to buy another one. There are brown ones, two-tone ones and a pair for 2500 euros. 2500 euros is the price of a year's worth of sessions or twice that. The dream brings back a memory: her grandmother told her that, when she was a child and her grandmother tried to put shoes on her, white shoes, B. threw them away and said: "I want my mother". The memory of the discarded shoes sheds light on the repetition in the form of "throwing away /blaming oneself for not having" and reveals the substitution of the shoe for the lost mother.

We could count the major elements that are connected, disconnected and reconnected in dreams, in an infinite number of combinations, marked by colour guiding substitutions. Colour is also injected into her art; she has started painting.

B.'s treatment makes great use of symbolism. The work of symbolisation is carried out through several stages, through the joint mobilisation of several series of elements that progressively become significant, after a journey of successive differentiations and oppositions. B. is first identified with an undead person, a condensation of the dead child who "caused" her mother's death and of her mother's mourning as unfulfilled. The shoe occupies a preponderant place and its appearances reflect its trajectory as a symbol/symptom that ties her to the death of her mother and to the unfulfilled mourning. It is charged with the traits conferred on it by the impulse and which take on the aspect of different colours. At the same time, cyphers 1, 2, and 3 mark the different movements of separation, opposition and reunion that are imprinted on the objectal relations. The progression from 1 to 2 and then to 3 follows the milestones through which the treatment progresses at the same time as it denotes the appearance of the members of the family scenario.

The symptom follows a path similar to that highlighted by Lévi-Strauss in relation to the Oedipus myth. There, myth emphasised a drive trait through the use of symbols, the tools mediating between contradictory terms: the belief in man's autochthony on the one hand, and in the birth from the union of a man and a woman on the other hand. The symbol "shoe", extracted from the infantile scene that links it to the impossible mourning of the mother, comes to mark successively, through dreams, the different stages of its symbolisation. It accompanies the journey of contradictory terms, especially of black/white opposites in different scenes, to finally come to be linked to mourning. Black is identified as a trait indexing masochistic identification with the dead mother.

A symbolism that could be described as universal is used here but in a very personal way, accompanied by *ad hoc* language creations. The same could be said about the choice of the symbol "shoe". The shoe conveys colours that are themselves charged with affect. But the shoe can also be considered as a metonymy of the foot that mythical thought has not yet separated. It is explicitly associated with "jouissance", it is a symbol of jouissance, a jouissance to be converted into desire. This is what is achieved through the *metaphor of the brown "Converse"*, which opens the way to remembrance at the same time as that of the mourning of the mother. The work of symbolisation finally finds a new way out, on the side of sublimation, a hitherto unseen symbolic form, through a new investment, painting, a practice associated with the dead mother, a trait of the dead mother.

Notes

1 D. Boukhabza, *La lettre du rêve, un lecteur pour la psychose,* erès/Arcanes, 2012.
2 Please refer to Chapter 2, the mirror of dreams.
3 W.Apollon, D.Bergeron, L.Cantin, *After Lacan, Clinical Practice and the Subject of the Unconscious*, State University of New-York Press, 2002.
4 C.Kolko, *Les absents de la mémoire, Figures de l'impensé*, érès, 2004.
5 Celeste Labaronnie, Matias Laje, Gabriel Lombardi, *Relationships Between Dreams and Psychosis: Historical, Evolution and Present Moment*, l'Evolution psychiatrique, 85, 4, Oct.-Dec.2020.
6 D. Boukhabza, Dela voix au rêve, du rêve au sinthome, Apertura, Vol.7, 1992.
7 J. Lacan, J. Lacan, *À la mémoire d'Ernest Jones: Sur sa théorie du symbolisme* (1960) Écrits, Paris, Seuil, 1966.
8 J. Lacan, *Le Seminaire*, L'identification (The identification), unpublished.
9 Or of the mana function, that of opposing the absence of meaning without itself having any particular meaning, to speak like Lévi-Strauss.
10 These pathways are the Jungian counterpart of Freud's pathways out of narcissism. As we have seen it, for Freud, idealisation, a process that deals with the object, is a substitute for initial narcissism. It increases the demands of the ego and goes in the direction of repression, whereas sublimation, which does without it, provides another way out.
11 D.Boukhabza, *Le cas Jung, Aperçu sur la face psychotique du transfert*, Anthropos/Economica, 2017.
12 C.G.Jung, *The Red Book*, Liber Novus, S. Shamdasani (ed.), Philemon series & W.W. Norton & Co, 2009.
13 S. Freud, *Inhibition, Symptom and* Anxiety, SE, Vol. XX.
14 *Ibid.*
15 Freud adds the following about another case: "However, it should be pointed out that the representation of devouring by the father is part of a typical and archaic fund of childhood, and the analogies that could be drawn from mythology (Kronos) or from the life of animals are universally known".
16 It is not certain that the fear of devouring should be referred to the father rather than the mother.
17 J. Laplanche, *Problématiques II, Castration-Symbolisations (Issues II, Castration –Symbolisations)*, PUF Quadrige, 1998.
18 It is difficult not to mention the words of Hans' own father, Max Graf, himself a disciple of Freud: "On the occasion of my son's third birthday, Freud brought him a rocking horse which he himself rode up thefour flights of stairs to my house … ". Freud himself may not be a stranger to the emergence of phobia.
    Entretienavec Kurt Eissler (Interview with Kurt Eissler), *Bloc-notes de la psychanalyse*, 14, 1996).

Bibliography

Apollon, W., D. Bergeron, and L. Cantin, *After Lacan, clinical practice and the subject of the unconscious*, State University of New-York Press, 2002.

Boukhabza, D., *De la voix au rêve, du rêve au sinthome*, Vol. 7, Apertura, 1992.

Boukhabza, D., *La lettre du rêve, un lecteur pour la psychose*, Arcanes/érès, Toulouse, 2012.

Boukhabza, D., *Le cas Jung, Aperçu sur la face psychotique du transfert*, Anthropos/Economica, 2017.

Eissler, K., *Entretiens*, Bloc-notes de la psychanalyse, 14, 1996.

Freud, S., *Inhibition, symptom and anxiety*, Vol. XX, SE, 1926.

Jung, C. G., *The Red Book*, Liber Novus, S. Shamdasani (ed.), Philemon series & W.W. Norton & Co, 2009.

Kolko, C., *Les absents de la mémoire, Figures de l'impensé*, érès, 2004.

Labaronnie, C., M. Laje, and G. Lombardi, *Relationships between dreams and psychosis: historical evolution and present moment*, l'Evolution psychiatrique, 85, 4, Oc.t-Dec. 2020.

Lacan, J., *Le Séminaire*, L'identification, unpublished.

Lacan, J., *To Ernest Jones: On his Theory of Symbolism, Ecrits*, The First Complete edition in English, W.W. Norton & Co, 2006.

Lacan, J., *À la mémoire d'Ernest Jones: Sur sa théorie du symbolisme* (1960) Écrits, Paris, Seuil, 1966.

Laplanche, J., *Problématiques II, Castration-Symbolisations*, PUF Quadrige, 1998.

Conclusion

The treatment of psychoses has provided us with our first starting point. Our clinical practice has demonstrated how the work of dreams and their symbols can counteract delusion and promote the advent of the subject. This is also what steered us towards the path and work of C.G. Jung, exiled from the field of psychoanalysis after his break with Freud. We wanted to confront Freud's and Jung's thoughts to examine more closely the points of convergence as well as the differences and to extend the interrupted debate. The question had nevertheless been posed: is the symbol on the side of the symptom, the sexual and repression or on the side of the archaic and the collective? The Freud–Jung dispute turned out to have its source, or at least one of its sources, in the elaboration of different fields. The hyper-symbolism of schizophrenia has demonstrated the function of symbols in this case: a palliative function for the defect of primordial identification. Symbols provide support in through the collective symbolism, in the absence of a trace of the subject's history and an inscription of that trace. Delusion produces a short-circuit from the trace to the symbol which forecloses the trait, that is, the mark of the subject and support of the identification. The analytical treatment favours the emergence of dream sequences, realising the writing of the traces of an individual history starting from the exercise of the symbolic, collective function. The writing of dreams transforms these traces into traits, inscribing the trace of the subject. From the collective symbolism, a trait can then be recognised by the subject as belonging to the other. In the field of neurosis, symbols have another function. Under the action of censorship, the symbol becomes a symptom, a symbol of the trauma, but deprived of its symbolic efficacy, that of associating with other symbols. It has fixed and ciphered the drive trait, borrowing the form of primitive thought to which it remains linked: the animal totem of phobia, the taboo of obsessional neurosis and the representation of the body in hysteria. But symbols are also the operators of the deciphering of the symptom, *via* dreams. Symbols are the tools of regression as well as of progression, of deciphering as well as of ciphering. They are a primitive modality of representation or rather *the first modality of representation*, that is connected to the image. They are similar to the residues of a pictographic or hieroglyphic writing, awaiting the passage to another form of writing—the transliteration that dreams produce. The passage to speech through the enunciation of the dream, tearing up and deciphering the image, makes the trait appear. The ambiguity of the symbol, in order to be lifted, requires the reunion of its two faces: the image and the trait. The image reveals that it bears the trait. The symbol can then be reduced to the trait, that is, a unary trait resulting from the relation to the other and representing the subject in this system of solidary signs that is language. Is the symbol able to reduce the opposition neurosis-psychosis? In other words, can the symbol be conceived not only as a way out of narcissism but as the only way out? In the end, the Oedipus complex would only be one symbol among others, dependent on a particular social organisation at a particular moment in history. The Freudian path of sublimation, which does without repression, is similar to the Jungian individuation process. Sublimation, this process concerning the drive that chooses a goal other than sexual, proves to be a practicable path for psychosis. It proceeds from the libido withdrawn from the object, but *to the point of denying this origin*, that is, its borrowing from the other; its source needs to be recognised as the result of transference and the re-actualisation of the object relation. The path of symbolisation then joins that of sublimation, but a sublimation that would not do without the object relation. The Ego-ideal of the neurotic also requires this sublimation without being able to produce it. The exit of neurosis implies the giving up of the idealisation of the ego as well as that of the object and the relaunch of the process of symbolisation; the outcome of the creation is to be expected at the end of an analysis.

Anthropology has provided us with a second point of departure. Myth expresses the fundamental themes of human life and translates them into various scenarios. The identification with a drive trait of the myth constitutes the spring of its effectiveness for the collective thought in the same way as it does for psychosis; symbols are the representative of the drive in dreams as in myths. Myths, like dreams, result from a work of a reading–writing of the drive that needs to be deciphered; they conceal the traits or qualities resulting from the dynamics of the drive and its different destinies. The subject can see himself in them as in the series of the image symbols that have organised his history constituting a symbolic universe whose laws must be recognised. All the variants of the myth can be ordered in a series forming a group of permutations mediating between contradictory terms. In the individual, the organisation of dreams into series around certain words or themes has an identical function. The movements of inversion or opposition, typical of the symbolic function, are found in the isolated dream as well as in its seriation, which is a law of development orders. The intersection of the series, juxtaposing elements that were previously separated, is capable of bringing back a key memory whose elements had escaped symbolisation and which the progression and the crossing of the series make it possible to recover. Symbolic memory not only repeats the experience of the past, but it also reconstructs it. The process of symbolisation activated by dreams involves, first of all, figuration which binds together word and thing and allows for the identification of a trait through the confrontation of elements presenting similarities. However, the seriation of dreams goes a step further: it commands the production of variations from one element or a configuration of several elements, progressing together like a group of transformations. The seriation of dreams installs an ordering according to differential values, linking the terms of the series, as well as the series themselves, together. Through the series, the element that has become recurrent detaches itself from the object to represent the subject. The seriation brought into play by dreams draws out the subject's own trajectory; it indicates the evolution of its relationship to those objects that have become its privileged objects. The symbolic function is the place of the confrontation of opposites and ties up or unties oppositions. It overhangs the process of the constitution of the subject and the organisation of its symptoms, going beyond the individual-collective opposition. The collective symbolism in psychosis lacks the inscription of the trait which is the index of the subject's passage. In neurosis, the trait remains encysted, unelaborated in typical dreams. The symptom presents itself as a residue of the collective history to be elaborated, a residue of primitive thought where the God/father has not yet been reduced to a trait. Located in the place where the God/father was, the symbolic function is what avoids the cult of the father as well as that of the organisation of crowds and its ideal.

The history of the religious function reveals the different stages of the alliance uniting the symbol with the group and made it possible to grasp the place of this function in the psychic structuring of man, particularly at the time of the separation of the religious from its mythical foundation. The divine first illuminated everything that seemed to be out of the ordinary, everyday life. It then became attached to human activity, to finally personalise and characterise itself with the different traits resulting from the previous periods. A process of naming followed step by step this evolution and put the word in relation to the creator god as an instrument or a foundation from which he himself proceeded. Monotheism came to complete the process in a movement of reversion with the unity of the concept of god, which became a god without name or properties. The mythico-religious stamp adheres to language and imprints its use. The passage from myth to religion is the consequence of the movement of extraction of the subject from the lack of differentiation between the subject and the object; it is contemporary with the emergence of the question of meaning, carried by language. A boundary gradually appears between representation and perception, between wish and fulfilment and between image and thing. The advent of subjectivity passes through religion as an essential stage and can be fixed there in variable ways for the individual and the group. The pleromatic conception of the divine, extracted by Jung from the gnosis of the early

Christian era, also bears the imprint of the history of the religious function. The divine world is made up of a set of qualities, coexisting in the form of pairs of opposites which cancel each other out through their opposition; the task assigned to the Creature is to differentiate them. It is by differentiating and reconciling the opposites that man, as a Creature, separates himself from the divine and denounces his totalitarian character. The differentiation of qualities and the mediation of opposites is the condition of any separation from the totalitarian, divine or not. Deconstructing the god, the object, the other, and withdrawing its omnipotence by discriminating its attributes, is what allows one to emancipate oneself from it. This is the task devolved to the subject.

The distinction made by Cassirer between different symbolic forms underlines the process of symbolisation in the social group. The emphasis is on a movement, a direction of meaning. The development of this process is accompanied by the emergence of the subject which takes place in parallel. Symbolisation is a dynamic process through which the relations between subject and object are constantly manifested and modified, as are the boundaries that separate them from each other. Yet, mythical thought, an unconscious thought, is persistent. Language is constantly connected to it, but itself pursues another, discriminative, direction, which will continue and amplify in scientific thought, without any solution of continuity. The persistence of mythical, unconscious thought constantly modifies the subject/object boundaries and regularly induces in the social group the prevalence of idealised or even deified collective objects, and sometimes scientific ones. The symbolic function is called upon to limit and regulate the relationship to these objects as well as to mark out the place of each individual, one by one, within the different groups to which he or she belongs: family, institution, state etc. as links in a whole to which each individual must relate singularly. We find these three symbolic forms, myth, language and knowledge, also at work in the dream as a transitional symbolic form itself. The mythical façade of dreams is worked on by language and it is language that allows the separation from myth to which it is intertwined in dreams, as it was for primitive thought. The analytical treatment will give a considerable extension to this work of disentanglement. But that is not all, it is also a quest for knowledge that dreams trigger and develop, like a true embryology of knowledge. Symbols of collective use will be marked with the seal of the subject. New elements, hitherto undifferentiated, will be discriminated and named. The mobilisation of the subject, highlighted by the seriation of dreams, constitutes the marker of the effectiveness of the analytical treatment and is perhaps the most capable of demonstrating its scientific character.

Index

Page numbers followed by "n" indicate notes.

For Product Safety Concerns and Information please contact our EU
representative GPSR@taylorandfrancis.com
Taylor & Francis Verlag GmbH, Kaufingerstraße 24, 80331 München, Germany

www.ingramcontent.com/pod-product-compliance
Lightning Source LLC
Chambersburg PA
CBHW050614280326
41932CB00016B/3040